To: Alice Masters
In memory of those
silenced before their time
Elly Gross, née Berkovits
December 03, 2008

Storm Against the Innocents

Holocaust Memories and Other Stories

By Elly Gross, née Berkovits

Some poems which appear in this book have been published previously in variation in "Poems of Elly Gross, Memories of a Holocaust Survivor," © 2000, Elly Gross

Library of Congress Control Number: 2003097136

ISBN 0-9713639-1-9

Printed in Canada

Table of Contents

I wrote these narratives and poems between 1966-2001 in memory of my parents, brother, and all other victims who lost their lives due to hate and prejudice. Some are about my family's life prior to the Second World War; others are personal experiences during the Holocaust and after. In 1998, 1999, and 2000 I returned to Auschwitz-Birkenau and visited Majdanek, Sandomirz and Tykochin. Again in 2001 I witnessed terrorism, this time in the U.S.A.

Part Two: Afterthoughts-
New Stories and Poems

THE WHITE HOUSE

Mrs. Elly Gross

Thank you for your kind gesture and for your special remembrance. Your expression of friendship means a great deal to us, and we send you our best wishes.

Laura Bush

Peace on Mother Earth

It would be nice for every living person to live in peace on our Mother Earth. It does not matter what color or religion. Every person has equal rights to create an existence with every opportunity he has.

Some people create miseries for themselves and other fellow human beings. In blind hate, without thinking, they destroy their own lives and every living person in their path. Why can no one stop them before they act? The ants live in large communities. They work together in peaceful ways. The bees carry the flowers' sweet juice to their common nest in a large group. They work as a family together. Why can't people learn from ants and bees? To work together or at least tolerate other fellow human beings' religion and ways, so they can flourish peacefully on Mother Earth. Why is it human nature to destroy others? Hate, prejudice and fist fights do not solve differences; they only create destruction.

In the New Millennium, I wish that every person should prosper and live in peace. Then the new generation can have a good life. I wish that the next generation should never have war, always live in peace, and love one another on our Old Mother Earth.

Letters

Elly Gross, Our Mother

My mother had me soon after she returned from the concentration camp. She was fifteen when the Hungarians and Germans took her away. She returned after the terrible ordeal to find her parents and her brother gone. She returned to her home to find it occupied by some strangers who then proceeded to chase her away.

Mom dreamed of going to school, but she needed to find a home. She met my dad, who was eight years older, and got married at seventeen. She skipped her teenage years; she never had time to develop into an adult. She struggled together with her husband, also a survivor, to forget and start a new life.

My father was a farmer before the war, but when the Communists took over he had to give the land to the collective and take a government job in the next village. He was always at work, and Mom was lonely and always kept me close to her. I was her ray of sunshine, her beautiful little bright doll, the doll she was unable to have as a child. She spoiled me: I got the best toys my parents could afford, the only tomato in the house, the prettiest clothes that could be found. At the same time, Mother wanted me to be strong, to know about life. She wanted me to read at four, learn to sew at five, and learn to cook when I was six. I was sick a lot and our village did not have a doctor. The school had only four grades that were taught by one teacher, in one large room. Mom was determined to move to the city, where there were better schools and good medical care, but the Communist Party forbade anyone to move there unless he had a house and a job. After my brother was born and I once again became very ill, Mother somehow managed to get a job in the city. We moved to the house my parents were building there, but it had only one room finished. Dad had to stay behind for another year until he was able to get a job as well. I always remember Mother striving to achieve her goals and never taking "no" for an answer if there was any stone to still be turned.

I don't remember at what age I became aware of the horrible ordeal my parents went through during the Holocaust and at what age I saw the first book describing those horrible experiments that Dr. Mengele conducted on the prisoners. I just know that at some point in my life my mother showed a book to me and explained why she did not have her parents or brother. It was a while before I understood that she felt guilty because she was unable to save her young mother.

Mother had few friends, and they were all survivors, all older than she, because she was one of the youngest who survived the camps. I was amazed by the fact that all these survivors managed to function, have children, go to the theater, care about life, after the ordeal they went through.

There was always the shadow of anti-Semitism around us. Our house had to be spotless, our appearance had to be neat, and we did not want to be literally "dirty Jews." I also felt the need to make amends to my parents. I needed to help around the house and I had to be a good student; they had suffered enough.

Later my family moved to the United States and Mother went on to do the things that survivors do. Together with her husband she achieved the American Dream. Mother got a high school education, helped her husband build a business, buy a house and a car. Her children went to college and started successful careers. She had grandchildren who in turn went on to good colleges and are starting great careers. Mother got a college degree at the age of sixty-nine. She was the oldest student in her classes.

Now she has found her purpose in life. She will not let people forget the atrocities; she will teach young people that prejudice of all kinds is wrong, teach that discrimination and violence is wrong. She has gone on the March of the Living with young people several times. She travels to schools all over the country to speak to students and writes books to convey her message.

My mother, Elly Gross, is not only a survivor; she is also an achiever.

Agneta Weisz

Elly Gross, My Mother

I was lucky to be born ten years after Mother came back from the concentration camp. She was not very healthy when I was born; she had a severe respiratory infection. I later learned that she had worked as a slave in a factory plant. My sister also became severely ill when I was two years old, so Mom had to be away for months with her at the hospital. After my sister got better, we moved to the city and I had sheltered life. My family loved me and took care of me.

I was ten years old when my family moved to the United States, and for years I saw my parents very little. They worked at two, three jobs and went to night school to learn English.

Mother continued on in school and proceeded to get her high school diploma. Then she took more courses so she would be able to get an office job. She was always trying to better herself and help her family prosper. She encouraged Dad to get into a business and left her office job to help him. My parents' hard work encouraged me by example and enabled me to get an education.

I am very proud of my mother's accomplishments. She is a great inspiration not only to me, but to all young people. Having been orphaned at the age of fifteen, she managed to create a good life for her family. But that was not enough for her. She now wants to leave a legacy and try to change the world. By letting people read about her experiences, she tells them what discrimination leads to. She not only gives her time when she speaks in schools all over the country about her experience and against prejudice, but donates all proceeds from her books to charity.

My mother is a special woman.

Tiberiu A. Gross

Elly Gross, Our Grandmother

To merely call Elly Gross an impressive woman is such an understatement. Though she lost almost her entire family to the great evil of the century, though she endured the life of a slave laborer in a filthy factory, she survived. She returned home to nothing in Romania, but married a man named Ernest and began a life and family. They eventually left Romania and the communist regime there and moved to New York City. Not really able to speak the language, Elly and Ernest Gross again began with nothing. Eventually they came to own their own business, for which Elly managed the books. While they were able to provide educations for their children, they were too busy to do so for themselves. Much later, after retirement, she went on to get an Associate's degree with major in Fine Arts from LaGuardia College. But just educating herself was not enough. She began speaking at schools about her experiences, to ensure that the horror of just over fifty years ago would not be forgotten. She was a plaintiff in a lawsuit against the company that callously used her and so many others as slave laborers. Even before the lawsuit began, she promised any compensation to charity. She went on trips such as The March of the Living, in which she helped to ensure that young people truly understood just what her experiences were at the sites where they had happened.

As her grandson, I (along with, of course, my brother) was a welcome overnight guest at my grandparents' house every weekend. In the evening and morning she always asked, "What can I make for you?" though she often said, "When I was sixteen..." late at night. I remember when my grandmother retired, and she challenged herself with college at the same time I did. I remember her triumph when she succeeded. I was born well after her great trial, but through her stories I know about much of what she experienced, and I will remember. So will everyone who reads this book.

Gabriel Weisz

Elly Gross, née Berkovits has always led a life of many roles, rapidly metamorphosing from student to prisoner of war, from freed slave to bride, from housewife to business woman, from mother to caretaker. Throughout all these roles, one characteristic remained constant. Elly Gross is a Survivor, of war which shattered all of the nations and conventions of Europe, of the atrocious death camps where "undesirables" were swept away, and of the ensuing struggle after the war to regain a foothold in normal society. She is a survivor of the turmoil of the communist regime in Romania and of the flight from there to a hopeful land of opportunity. Elly's unique, unbreakable spirit upheld her through triumph and tragedy and enabled her to bring her children to realize the fullest potential of the American Dream. Now, she spends her time taking care of her husband, who unfortunately suffered a stroke several years ago, and bullying her various descendants with reflections sprinkled with her perspectives on the tragedies of modern years. In her immigrant's simple yet powerful language, she lets us share the voyage through the most troubled years of the century and allows us to feel, on a very fundamental level, the powerful nobility of that unusual creature, the Survivor.

Her grandson, Jonathan Weisz

Aishet Chayil, A Woman of Valor

I met Elly Gross some years ago when she asked to be included as a Holocaust survivor on the March of the Living, a program designed to bring Jewish youth on a two week odyssey through Jewish history in Poland and Israel. Her mission, as she perceived it, was to educate these youngsters about what happened to the Jewish people in Europe prior to and during World War II. By referring to her own story, she was able to transmit the truth and the horrors about man's inhumanity to a people of a certain religion and ethnicity. She participated in several of those journeys and continues to speak to young people in every school setting to make them aware of a period of history that they can only find in a few chapters in history books.

She has not forgotten one iota of her past history in Europe and has taken to writing books of poignant poetry in memory of her family, in some instances, personally paying for their publication. Additionally, any profits from the sale of those slim volumes have been earmarked for special projects in Israeli hospitals.

In spite of or because of what she endured, Elly Gross has evolved into a true Woman of Valor, a priceless human being intent upon doing her part to ensure that the Shoah…the Holocaust…will never be forgotten.

Susan Rachlin, Board of Jewish Education (Retired), Director of Special Projects
March 2003

Elly Gross, My Friend

Elly Gross with her heart steeped in loving kindness and her creative energy cutting a searing path through our emotional quietude. Elly, who tells her stories in a curious monotone, with dispassionate demeanor in her heavy Romanian accent, stories that are so filled with bone-chilling horror that it is a miraculous blessing that she is a gentle, forbearing soul.

She cooks delicious, fresh food, paints beautiful botanical oils, writes poems into the wee hours of the night and recounts the extremes of human sufferings inflicted by savage sadists in the short stories set forth in this lovely book.

Elly is a wise historian, a recent graduate of LaGuardia College, care-giver to her ailing husband and a frequent guest of the Holocaust Museum. She travels from classroom to classroom teaching children about the travails of the Jews during World War II. To keep the memory alive so that her life has a deeper purpose, she published this book at her own expense. Her fierce desire is to have the tales outlive the teller.

Elly Gross is remarkable, my sweet, talented beloved friend.

Lois Silverman, Chief Executive Manager
Milberg Weiss Bershad Hynes & Lerach LLP

Introduction

Elly Gross came into my office in the winter of 1998 bearing a smile on her sweet face; a smile I later realized is permanently affixed to cloak the unimaginable remembrances of a past so horrible that they transcend our ability to comprehend. This Holocaust survivor, at the age of fifteen, was transported from her home in Şimleul-Silvaniei, Transylvania, with her thirty-seven year old mother and five year old brother to Auschwitz—by cattle car. On their arrival they were unloaded, with hundreds of others, only to be separated—one group to the left the other to the right—by a Nazi officer wearing white gloves. Elly later learned that officer was Dr. Josef Mengele, the infamous Nazi doctor who used human beings as medical guinea pigs. Elly wound up on the right, her mother and brother on the left. Elly never again saw them alive.

After surviving over a year in several concentration camps, including Auschwitz, and working as a slave laborer at a Volkswagen plant, Elly was freed by the Allies and went back to Romania, married, had a son and daughter, and later moved to the United States. Fifty years later, she participated, with teenagers from the United States, in the March of the Living, visiting Auschwitz and walking with the youths to the site of the murders, where she saw photographs of vicious images that she has endured every day of her life, those of the concentration camp and her life as a slave laborer. But, a particular photograph stood out among the others. First she spotted the white gloves that by a wave to the left separated her forever from her loved ones. Then Elly was thunderstruck by the picture of her mother, holding her young brother in her arms, standing in front of the railroad cars, surrounded by hundreds of other prisoners. Rendered speechless, numbed by the vision that she thought she would carry forever only in her memory, Elly went home and started to write. She spoke little, but wrote much. She wrote poems which I published for her.

Now she has written stories as moving and powerful as her poetry. Elly undertook to publish them herself because of how deeply she cares about creating a lasting monument to those who suffered and survived—or didn't survive. Here are her stories.

Melvyn I. Weiss,
Milberg Weiss Berhard Hynes & Lerach LLP

Part One

Short Stories and Poems

My Mother's Flowers

My mother loves flowers
and plants them every spring.
Her morning glory
climbs on a string.
With green leaves
and colorful flowers,
the morning glory makes
shadows on our open hallway.

My mother loves
the Japanese lily;
it blooms with white flowers,
with strong fragrance.
My mother loves the dahlia;
some name it "the pauper flower,"
with its bright colored flowers,
open late summer into autumn.

The Author's Mother, Irina Berkovits
(1906-1944)

Mother loves zinnias too,
in rainbow colors,
all-summer sprouting,
cutting flowers.

My mother also likes portulaca.
It grows in sand or stone,
and blooms as a colorful blanket
covering the ground.

Another of my mother's favorites
is the rooster head.
The flowers are dark red
and bloom all summer.

My mother loves
every flower in any color.
In her small garden,
flowers always bloom.
Mother takes care of
her beautiful flowers,
and the air is filled
with fragrance.

I Went to Kindergarten

With a blue bow in my hair and a lunch bag in my hand, I went to the kindergarten on a windy, cloudy day. As I got close to the nursery a little rain sprinkled. But I was not too wet as I walked into the long hallway. Another girl entered with an umbrella in her hand. My umbrella was home. I felt desperate. Standing on my toes, I opened the door, and in the pouring rain ran out crying, to return home through the pouring rain.

My parents' neighbor's son saw me on the rainy street. He asked "Why are you crying? What is wrong?" Sobbing hysterically, I explained that one girl came with an umbrella to kindergarten. And I did not have one, so I had to return home to bring my umbrella. He took me home in his arms.

I will never forget this episode as long as I live. How foolishly a child's mind works! Already arrived at the nursery, crying, I ran out in the rain and got soaking wet for an umbrella. Soon the rain stopped and the sun shone in the blue sky.

What a silly child I was. Mother changed my wet clothes. Smiling, she put me into bed, and I cried bitterly as I fell asleep.

The Author at two years old.

My Hometown

I remember Şimleul-Silvaniei, where I was born, as a beautiful city. The city lies in a valley, surrounded by the Meses Mountain. All year round there is snow on the mountain.

I remember, in the summer when it rained, or when the sun shone very bright, some snow melted. The city's river, the Crasna, rapidly rose, overflowing its banks. Muddy water covered the left side of my hometown. People packed and moved to higher ground. The muddy water swept away everything in its path.

I lived on the right side of the river by the Magura Hills. From the High Hills of the Magura, a small stream with crystal clear water flowed slowly down the middle of my street. In the middle of the paved street, in the summer's warm weather, my friends and I dammed the water with sand, to create our own lake. We floated our paper boats on the lake. Proud "sailors" made from matches navigated the boats on our lake. Those paper boats soaked and soon sank. The one whose boat went under first was the loser in that game.

Our fun turned sour when it rained or when the snow melted. The stream grew angry and big. Water covered our street from one side to the other, carried stones and broken trees.

When it got cold the water froze, and created a frozen street from side to side. We children hurried to go on the ice. Our mothers worried that we children would get frostbite. It never bothered us.

My Only Doll

Twice a year, with Mother, we visited my grandmother. Granny lived in another town, so she seldom had a chance to see us. Her other seven grandchildren visited her almost every day. And as some grandmothers do, she criticized them for everything.

Grandmother loved me a lot, but she never gave me a gift. In the 1930's, very few could spend money on presents. Families could not buy gifts or toys. They were satisfied to make ends meet. We children created our toys from wild chestnuts, matches, beans, ropes, strings, wild flowers, and stones.

Once, when my friend's father traveled, he brought my friend furniture for dolls. Although my father always worked, he had no money for presents or toys. One time my father traveled too, and he brought me a beautiful doll. I was happy and felt "in heaven." She had a porcelain face and blond hair.

I ran to my friend with my new gift, and suggested that we should play with her furniture and my doll. She said, "Let me see your doll." I put my beautiful doll in her hand. Then she hit it on the side of a wood barrel and broke my only doll's nose.

Devastated as I was, I ran home crying. Mother said, "If you do not like that she broke your doll's nose, do not play with her anymore." Mother was smart!

Next day, we played together again. We tried to repair the doll's nose. My friend was a doctor and I was a nurse. We could not repair the broken nose. I never got another doll. As I aged, I realized, I never had a truly good friend.

My First Dancing Class

My aunt's younger brother opened a dancing school for teenagers. With a few of my friends we registered for classes. We learned how to dance gracefully and not step on our partners' toes.

Some of my friends had prior dance instruction. For them it was easy to follow the music rhythm and dance gracefully. At my first dance lesson, I was a clumsy young child. Not many boys asked me for a dance.

My disappointment increased as heavy storm clouds darkened the sky. It thundered and lightning hit the dance hall. Electric wiring burned, and we were in complete darkness. Heavy rain with egg size hail covered the ground.

I was scared and miserable. I started to cry hysterically, "Please, someone help me get home to my mother." Who wants to walk in a heavy storm with a crying girl?

During the storm, hail over twenty centimeters thick—close to a foot—covered the ground. The heavy storm knocked out trees, electric and telephone lines. On streets, it was hazardous and difficult to walk. Ice covered the streets.

People shoveled hail for hours and made piles of ice. As the storm raged no one danced and everyone's time was ruined.

Cold and Icy Day

In my hometown, winter begins about October every year. First it's cold, rainy, and windy; then rain freezes on the street. It's treacherous to walk on icy roads. It does not matter, in rain or cold—the freezing weather does not stop children from going to school. Parents worry that their children might fall on the slippery paths.

In dangerous weather, parents walk their children to school. My father worried that I might fall, so he got ready to come with me to school on a cold, rainy, frozen day.

Frozen rain created ice on streets. To protect me, my father held a cane in one hand and with his other held my hand. He balanced himself with his cane. The street was shiny with frozen rain. Father slipped on the slippery ice and fell backwards on the ground. He hit his back and head hard. I tried to help him to get up, but he was big and I was small.

Crying, I asked people for help, but not many walked on the street. From the bakery across the street someone came to help my father up from the icy frozen street. Luckily my daddy got only bruises.

With no escort, I got to school. Our teachers dismissed classes early. The sun smiled and melted the ice. Soon there was none left on the street.

My Only Brother

I was a lonely single child and jealous of my friends, of those who had a brother or a sister with whom to play. I felt small and very alone. When I was ten years old, my little brother was born. He was handsome, with black hair, red cheeks and black eyes. I was happy to have a brother.

I loved the little boy and he liked to be with me. He took his first steps, balanced with his hands, and with a smile he ran into my arms. I felt so joyous that I cried. The boy was close to my heart. It gave me great satisfaction when our mother trusted my little brother to my care. I planned to go together with him to the park when he grew up and on the hills to pick wild strawberries, blackberries, and wild flowers for our mother. Our father also had plans for his only son's bar-mitzvah, the school the boy would attend. Maybe he would be a doctor, perhaps a lawyer or a mechanic.

In the spring, when my brother was born, the Nazis invaded Czechoslovakia. The winds of the Second World War began to blow over our heads, but no one could have imagined what followed next. Fate changed our family's life, and our dreams did not come true. In the stormy winds of Europe, our hopes were demolished, and again . . . I remained a single lonely child.

The Author's Brother, Adalbert Berkovits
(1939-1944)

The Storm that Struck Europe

Those who were born in the late 1920's or in the 1930's missed the prior, worry-free life. But the problem started much before, when the breeze of World War I began—it was in the early 1910's. Many people died during the war, and life afterwards was difficult. Depression rose high. Whose fault was it? Easy to blame a group of people.

Where to find a nation that can be blamed for a difficult and harsh life? It must be a nation without a homeland, a group of people who have no country, who cannot say, "We have a country, a homeland." This nation is free prey, and the Depression can be blamed on them. They have no country on earth to go to.

By blaming Jews in the 1920's and 1930's, a lunatic of the era united his people. The slogan, "Kill the Jews" was music to the Nazi and collaborator ears. In the storm that swept through Europe, Jews were such easy prey. No homeland, no country where Jews could go. In this storm my people were robbed of their possessions and their lives.

For the few of us who survived with broken hearts, our homeland, Israel is the cure for our destroyed lives. Small and strong, Israel is a beautiful country where we Jews can go to mend our broken hearts. Now we can say with heads held high and pride in our hearts, "We have a country. We have a homeland. We will not allow it to happen again—that Jews around the world be easy prey." We have the State of Israel, a place to go.

Hungarian Invasion

People in Europe were suffering; everyone was struggling. Depression is like the locust, that eats up everything in its path. As after fire, only bare ground remains. In the market there was plenty of food, but very few had money to buy. No work! No income! Even though life was harsh, we were home together, and we had our freedom.

Soon more problems arose. On September 10, 1940, the Hungarian invasion brought devastation to local people. The new government seized treasures, looted everything, took over the border to the mainland.

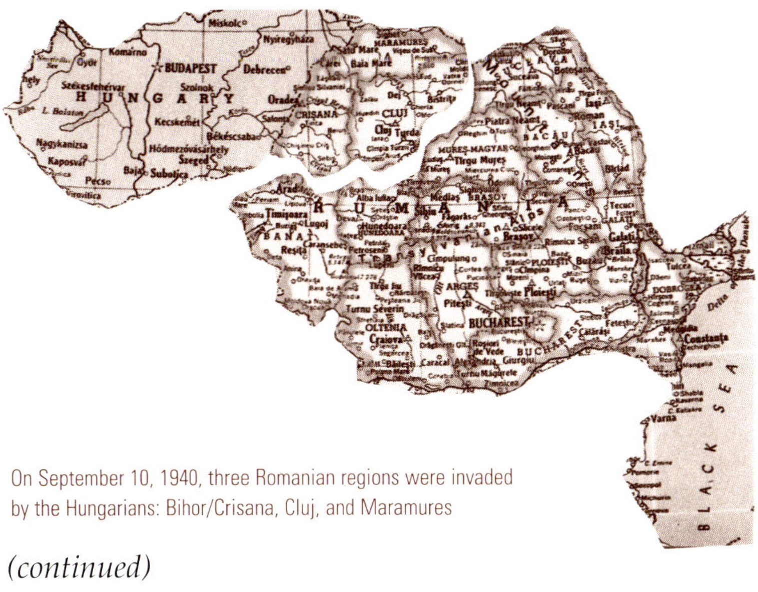

On September 10, 1940, three Romanian regions were invaded by the Hungarians: Bihor/Crisana, Cluj, and Maramures

(continued)

Life day by day got harder. From their homeland Hungarians brought misery. Coupons were distributed. Food, clothing, and shoes were given by ration only. And for the lack of goods, Jews were blamed. The government seized Jewish belongings and property and gave them free to loyal Hungarians. Local Hungarians were happy for a while, but they got greedy and demanded more.

Harsh new laws hit the Jews. Restrictions were issued for travel and schooling; curfews were implemented, men drafted into forced labor, and other injustices. Still the Hungarians were not content; they wanted more.

It was spring. It was warm. The sun was shining. Meadows were green. Trees and flowers were blooming, but for the Jews it was dark and cloudy.

To appease the locals and the Germans, the Hungarian government forced Jews out of their homes, out of their cities. And in a hurry, gave Jews to the Nazi Germans.

The Tenant Accused Me

Mommy seldom had to repeat that I should listen to adults. I tried to please the elders so they would not scold me. One day our tenant went to the market and bought a pair of chickens. She placed them across from her entrance in a sort of box which had small openings. As always, cats and dogs ran around the small yard. Maybe one touched the opening to the box so the chicks got out. The entrance to our apartment was on the other side of the building. I rarely used the back entrance. I did not even know the lady had chickens.

Late that afternoon she yelled at me and said, "You played with my chickens as if they were balls." At this time we were already under Hungarian jurisdiction. Mommy came and said, "Do not worry. I will pay for the chickens." She said this even though we did not have much money and she knew that I had been in school all day. At this time my father had already been taken away to forced labor.

Mommy knew I would not touch someone else's property. My dear mother was worried that this Hungarian tenant might go to the police and complain about me. Then who knows, they could put me in jail. The tenant made a lot of noise, and she screamed that she even had a witness who had seen me play with the chickens.

I was so scared, trembling, ready to pass out. Then from nowhere the chickens returned. They went into the box from which they had escaped earlier. The three of us just stood there. This unreliable Hungarian woman didn't say, "Sorry I accused you." She was Hungarian and we were Jews. Mommy said, "Thanks G'd, the chickens returned. Who cares for her apology; our worry is over."

This was our life under Hungarian rule.

Russian Hills

Beside Russian Hills,
a forced labor worker is marching.
Be careful, dear worker,
do not step on a mine.

Russians place mines
to protect their homeland.
The Hun-Magyars and the German Nazis
are invaders on Russian lands.

The Nazis draft Jews
into forced labor camps.
They make them walk through minefields,
and do not care how many die.

In one of these forced labor units
is my dear father, too.
I pray every day to G'd
that my father's life be saved.

Please, G'd, watch his unit.
Watch over my father,
so that he doesn't step on mines,
beside the Russian Hills.

To keep him warm I knit
sweaters and socks.
My mother prepares packages
to send to my father's unit.

We anxiously await a letter,
which never arrives.
How would we know that my father
received the warm clothes?

Please, G'd, take care of
all those in forced labor units,
and help them return to their homes,
from beside the Russian Hills.

Oh G'd, hear, listen to my prayers
and save my father's life.
Please look after my father
so that he won't step on a mine.

Over two years passed when I was told
that my father was burned alive.
With his fellow laborers he perished,
beside the Russian Hills.

The Author's Father, Eugen Berkovits
(1905-1943)

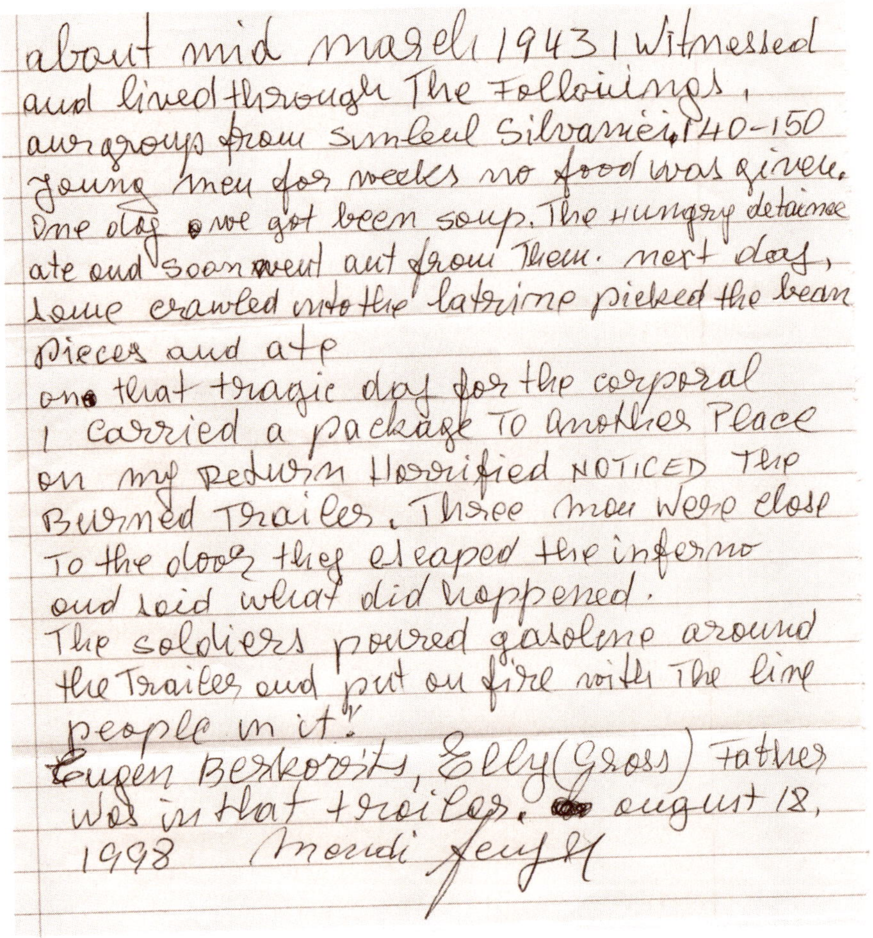

about mid march 1943 I witnessed
and lived through The Followings,
our group from Simleul Silvaniei, 140-150
young men for weeks no food was given.
One day we got been soup. The hungry detainee
ate and soon went out from Them. next day,
some crawled into the latrine picked the bean
pieces and ate
on that tragic day for the corporal
I carried a package To another Place
on my return Horrified NOTICED The
Burned Trailer. Three men were close
To the door they escaped the inferno
and said what did happened.
The soldiers poured gasoline around
the Trailer and put on fire with The live
people in it!
Eugen Berkovits, Elly (Gross) Father
was in that trailer. august 18,
1998 Mendi Feiger

About mid March 1943 I witnessed and lived through the followings. Our group from Şimleul-Silvaniei, 140-150 young men for weeks no food was given. One day we got been [bean] soup. The hungry detainee ate and soon went out from them. Next day some crawled into the latrine picked the bean pieces and ate. On that tragic day for the corporal I carried a package to another place. On my return horrified noticed the burned trailer. Three men were close to the door. They escaped the inferno and said what did happened. The soldiers poured gasoline around the trailer and put on fire with the live people in it. Eugen Berkovits, Elly (Gross) Father was in that trailer.

— August 18, 1998 Mendi Feiger

My Dear Daddy

My daddy was handsome; tall with black hair and black eyes. He loved me. Up to the age of ten I was his only child, whose looks resembled his late mother. His mother was pretty, with blue eyes, blonde hair, and a very light complexion. At an early age my daddy became an orphan. His father died in the First World War. Shortly after, his mother passed away.

The four handsome children remained in the care of their late father's brother. But the uncle sent the four boys away, and he took over their parents' house. The young boys traveled away from their village to find work. My daddy was fourteen years old, the eldest of the orphans. The four brothers learned tailoring, and their salary was their room and board.

Eventually two of Daddy's brothers escaped the misery they were in. The youngsters left for South America to start a new life in a strange land. The two brothers began to work, and then they opened a dry cleaning store. My Daddy's youngest brother soon followed the others to South America. Now the three brothers were together, and Daddy was struggling in the old land. In Europe, there was recession and no work. Then catastrophe fell on European Jews.

My dear father was drafted into a forced labor camp in June 1942. His group marched on foot with no food, no water, no shoes and no warm clothes. His keepers forced the group into a trailer, locked the doors and poured gasoline around the trailer. Then the sadistic soldiers put a match to the gasoline and burned them alive. My thirty-seven year old father was among the group of young men. G'd, why?

We forever miss my daddy, who, far from his family, suffered cold and hunger for months. And fire took my dear daddy's life.

Miss, Did a Star Fall on You?

After the Hungarian invasion of September 10, 1940, we Jews were deprived of citizens' rights. In 1944 the Hungarian Government issued a decree that we Jews must wear a yellow Star of David. With the yellow patch on our left chest we Jews were labeled with the Star of David. The local population could recognize a fearful Jew from far away on the city's street.

Locals called to us, "Dirty Jew—a star fall on you?" They freely spit on Jews, and some Jews were beaten. That I was born a Jew was a daily shame. Yesterday's friends asked: "Miss, did a star fall on you?" Even though I was the same Jewish child on our street with whom they had grown up and played for many years.

A question still remains: Did Jewish leaders know about the laws that were being made against the Jews? Jews daily had fewer and fewer citizens' rights.

No one ever will know how much our leaders knew.

Jewish women selected to labor
(Auschwitz-II-Birkenau, June 2, 1944)

We Made Matzo!

The Hungarian authorities forbade
Jews to make or import matzo.
Granny and her son outsmarted the law.
They called Granny's brother and they
figured how to make and bake matzo.
They washed the grain, then dried it
in the sun, and afterwards ground it.

There was plenty of flour for matzo.
Grandmother got new wood
and smoothed the wood with glass.
Then Grandmother gathered
the family to make the matzo.
Her brother made the dough
and we grandchildren rolled
it on the new wood table.

When we rolled the matzo dough,
the pieces that got wrinkled
were not kosher for Passover.
The boys gave the wrinkled dough
to the chickens in the backyard.
After rolling each ball of dough
we had to scrape the table
with a piece of clean glass.

When we rolled the matzo
we got blisters on our hands.
Grandmother and her brother heated
a large brick oven using chopped wood,
and the family helped
to make and bake the matzo.

Granny with her family outsmarted
the law Hungarians imposed on Jews.
Granny, her son, and brother helped
the family to have kosher matzo.
This was my family's last Passover.

The Knife with Mother of Pearl Handle

Sometime in the 1930's my uncle from South America came to visit his birthplace to see his mother, his sisters, brothers and other relatives. He was a handsome bachelor, who planned to get married. Many families wished that perhaps he would choose their daughter. Friends recommended many girls. Finally, one day he found a match. His fiancé was chic and pretty; Granny was happy.

At the wedding people danced on top of tables. The new couple sat me next to them, and they gave me two valuable presents: a two-inch narrow knife with a mother of pearl handle and a gold ring. The small knife became useful on field trips organized by my school. As Jews' lives in Europe got more miserable, the pocket knife became more useful and indispensable.

On a sunny day, May 27th 1944, Saturday, erev Shavuot* we were strip-searched in a tent in the Ghetto. I squeezed the small knife in my hand. We were forced into cattle cars without food or water. About ninety-five scared Jews, old men and women, young mothers with frightened hungry children. We did not even have air. In a corner, my mother, brother, and I were sitting between each others' legs. Then I began to make a hole with my knife in the cattle car wall.

Next day May 28th, 1944, early Sunday morning, the first day of Shavuot, the transport pulled into our hometown, into our city, for the last time. It was a sunny day and a holiday for gentiles also. The Hungarians came to the train station to see the locked cattle cars with the unfortunate Jews. The smiles and laughter on their faces is imprinted on my memory. That afternoon our transport began to roll. I made the hole bigger in the cattle car wall, so my mother, brother and I had fresh air. We were so desperate.

My five year old brother asked for water and food. Our mother held him tight. Mommy kissed him. She had no food or water to give to her son, but at least we had air.

*erev: the evening the holiday begins. Shavuot: (pronounced sheh voo' os or sheh voo'ot) Jewish holiday which celebrates harvest of the first fruits of the season.

Where Is G'd?

The sun shines bright,
but it is dark.
Smoke covers the sky,
so I can't see the sky.
Why is it so dark?

Ashes and fire arise
from the ground,
but there is
no fire around.

Oh yes, there are
five chimneys which
pour smoke with ashes
and darken the sky.

Goes up, up high in the air.
What could be there?
Heavy smell everywhere.
Is a rubber factory there?

Oh no, no,
my soul, my heart
goes to heaven.
Oh G'd, are you there?

Please open
the gate to paradise;
let my soul, my heart
enter heaven.

My heart breaks
and I ask why?
Where is our G'd?

The Death Gate at the railroad tracks.

June 2, 1944, as deportees, we arrived in Auschwitz-II/Birkenau. "Arbeit Mach Frei" translates to "Work Makes You Free."

The Echo and Chaos

I hear the echo of children's cries: "Mommy, I am hungry." "Do not cry, my child," Mother said. She holds and kisses her child, but she does not have any food or water to give to her child. Dogs on leashes bark, men in striped uniforms whisper, and soldiers scream: "Fast, fast, stinky Jew." Such chaos on the ramp. What is happening? Locked for six days without food and water, my mother holds in her arms my weakened brother.

A man in uniform with white gloves waves right and left, points my mother and brother to the left and me and others to the right. In the chaos, I ask, "When will I see my mother again?" A Kapo says, "Sunday at the family reunion." Over a year passed, and that Sunday never came. That blasted day of June 2, 1944, I waved goodbye to my mother and brother. The echo and chaos I hear and see every day as if it happened today.

On April 23, 1998, not Sunday, but Thursday, in Birkenau Lager D on a large display, a mother holds a child in her arms. And I see my mother, my brother. So I do have a family reunion. How can I reverse time to see them alive and try to go with them to the left? The echo and chaos forever ring in my ears. Can anyone understand my pain?

Auschwitz-II/Birkenau disembarkment ramp, June 2, 1944
The small boy and the woman holding him are are the Author's mother and brother.

Why Did I Not Say, "Mommy Please Come with Me"?

On May 27, 1944, my mother, brother and I were strip-searched, then forced into a boxcar with about 90 to 100 strangers, without food, water, or even air. The convoy of many boxcars started to roll. On Friday, June 2, 1944, the transport suddenly halted and the doors were opened.

Men in striped rags jumped into our boxcar. One whispered to me, "Say you are eighteen" and to my mother, "Give the boy to someone." I thought, "Are these men lunatics?" The men pushed old people and children. Sick and dead were thrown on the same truck. I thought, "What is wrong? Are they mad?"

Mother asked, "What should we do?" I said, "We cannot give my brother to strangers. He is five years old, and I am fifteen." It happened as fast as lightning; there was no time to think. I was pushed to the right.

(continued)

My mother, holding my brother in her arms, remained in the left line. As I ran to reach the others I waved to them. They looked in the direction in which I had departed. I relive this moment all my life.

During my life, as problems arise, it crosses my mind that I did wrong. I am tormented with remorse. Why did I not say to my mother, "Give my brother to anyone and come with me." Why do I feel guilt that mother was sent to the left?

In my life, tragedies poured on me. I was robbed of my father at age thirteen. When I was fourteen, he perished in a forced labor camp. When I was fifteen, my mother and brother were taken away from me. Was I selfish or not? Was what I did wrong?

If I could change the time I would not care that my brother was only five years old. I would say, "Mommy, give my brother to anyone." Why did I not say, "Mommy, please come with me"? You reader, be the judge. Why can I not forget? What punishment do I deserve? Was it my crime?

Symphony Music in Birkenau

On arrival to Birkenau from all countries, Jews heard soft music. An orchestra played a symphony. The players wore striped rags. They were pale, but they played beautifully on their instruments. The players were well known musicians in their respective countries.

When the musicians arrived in Birkenau they were selected for a special task. Their music was supposed to mislead and calm the newcomers to these killing fields.

As the long row of box cars rolled in, day and night with new deportees, the musicians played symphony music. SS soldiers and Kapos screamed, dogs barked, families separated, children cried, and men whispered. It was strange to hear the music. Those musicians greeted many victims to whom the symphony music was the last calming memory. It gave them some relief before they were murdered.

In the spring of 1944 in one month, about half a million deportees arrived. Large transports came, especially from Hungary and the other countries which were invaded by Hungarians. Jews came from the former Czechoslovakia, Serbia, and Romania's Transylvania. My family and I arrived from occupied Romania.

Since 1944 a question often comes to my mind about those who played music as new deportees arrived. Did any member of the orchestra survive the Holocaust? Did they testify about their misery, experience, and the selections?

The musicians lived through hell by knowing what the fate was of every person who was directed to the left. Selection to the right meant temporary survival for about one to two percent of the new arrivals.

(This is my true testimony; we were over 95 people squeezed in the cattle (box) car. In that car, a child was born; a few people died. At the last second only I was directed to the right.)

My Blond Ponytail

My hair was curly and golden blond.
It was long, down to my waist
and braided in two ponytails.
Mother boiled chamomile flowers
and washed my hair with love.

She brushed and braided my hair
every morning in two ponytails.
Then hell began to fall on Jews.
We were forced to the Ghetto.
Mother washed in cold water my hair.

She did not wash with chamomile my hair.
Mother didn't have warm water either.
Still long, down to my waist was my hair.
Mother brushed and braided with love
in two ponytails my golden blond hair.

Then we were forced in cattle cars.
Mother had no water to wash my hair;
Mommy had no brush to comb it.
Each morning, with her fingers,
she tried to comb and then braid my hair.

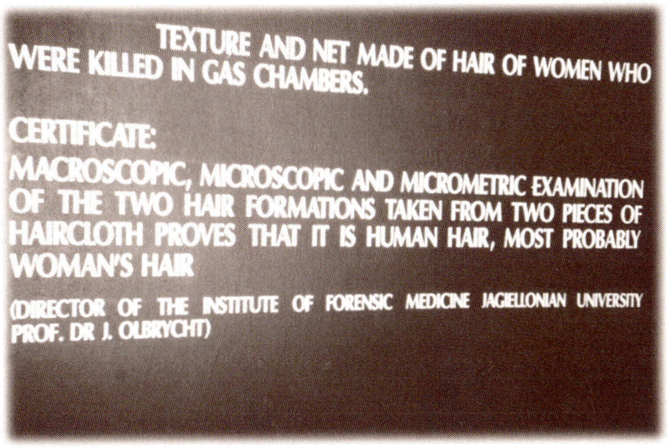

Then my mother was not there anymore.
I was alone. A girl cut my ponytails.
Then another girl came and shaved my head.
It is good mother did not see how
my long ponytails were put in a pile.

My long hair was golden blond; others'
were brown, black, and reddish. Our hair
was woven into blankets which were shipped
to Nazi SS officers' homes as bonuses.
In one blanket shines my blond hair.

Who is covered with the blankets made
from our hair? The hair in those blankets
asks, "Did any survive the living hell?"
At the age of thirty-seven my mother was
murdered. The gas turned her hair grey.

And her hair, with others who were
killed in the gas chambers,
turned grey from the Cyclon B gas.
Heads were shaved after death
and hair was used for mattresses.
Did the recipients ever know
the origin of the bonuses?*

*Faithful German citizens received items such as mattresses and blankets as bonuses for their loyalty.

Shower in Birkenau

A new train of deportees arrived and lined up in front of an officer. With a wave of his gloves he decided who should live and who should die. My group was sent to the right. We were not yet condemned to die. But most from our transport were directed to the left. We had been locked up for seven days without water and food, and we did not even have air.

Soldiers with rifles ready to shoot ordered us to line up, five in a row, and they held barking dogs on leashes. Men in striped uniforms helped the German soldiers to group us. We walked on a road between barbed wire. Our group arrived at a big building. Our escorts screamed, "Go inside! Fast!"

We entered a large hall with benches around the wall and numbered hooks. On the wall were signs written in German and in Hungarian: "Tie your shoes together. Remember your hook number, to find your clothes quickly." How organized the Germans were. What a lie it was. We did not know. None of us got our clothes back. Our folded clothes were sent to German citizens as bonuses.

Screaming soldiers watched us undress. Our heads were shaved. In the shower the water in one second was boiling hot and the next second it was changed to freezing cold.

We were thirsty; we were hungry. We stuck out our tongues to swallow a few drops of water. It did not matter if it was hot or cold. The Nazi Germans laughed. It was fun for them.

The First Food in Seven Days

Since Saturday morning May 27, 1944 seven days had passed. No food or water was in my mouth. The first moisture my body got was from the shower on the morning of June 2, 1944. Someone put a tiny piece of soap in my hand, and on it was written "Jude siefe" (Jewish soap). SS men watched us enter the shower room.

While water poured on my head I stuck out my tongue to swallow some drops. It did not matter if the water was hot or cold. My mouth was dry, my lips were cracked. It felt as if it would rejuvenate my tired body. At the shower there were no towels to dry ourselves.

After, our group, five in a row, was ushered to a wet and muddy road surrounded with double barbed wire. Every few meters were watch towers with soldiers ready to shoot. Screaming SS soldiers escorted us with rifles and barking German shepherds on leashes.

We arrived in a plaza, "Lager C." It was cold. We had wooden clogs on our feet, our bodies were only covered with a rag, with no underwear, socks or jackets. We were standing five in a row until it got dark. It rained as if the sky was crying for all of us. On my shaved head and my back it felt as if thousands of needles stuck my body.

(continued)

Late that day our group was escorted into a trailer with no beds. In our "Block 20," it rained through the roof. On the ground was knee-high muddy water. It was dark, crowded, and it was miserable. To keep ourselves warm we stood close to each other.

Late at night a large bucket of brown liquid was distributed in which some barley floated. We were told, "Everyone swallow three mouthfuls." It was boiling hot. The next person watched that the other should not swallow more. I swallowed three large mouthfuls. It was very bitter and so hot it burned my mouth. But who cared, my body got some nourishment for the first time in a week. We slept standing on our feet. We were exhausted. Slowly morning arrived. The overseer ordered us to run to the latrine, wash our face, and hurry for roll call. In a few weeks many young women got sick. They were selected and then taken away.

There Is No Bird or Butterfly

Barbed wire with high voltage
and watch towers with soldiers.
I can see only four tall chimneys,
which pour ash and fire.

The air is full of heavy smoke;
it smells like burned rubber.
I can never see the sun,
because the sky is blurry.

When the sun shines, it is still cloudy
and when it rains, the ground is muddy.
I walk on sand and stone.
There is no grass or tree.

If some green would grow,
without any shame,
I would pick it to eat—
even at the risk of being killed.

I am enclosed with my fellow inmates.
Our crime is that we were born Jews.
This place is forgotten
by everyone in the world.

The Nazis and collaborators
robbed us of everything:
our freedom, our possessions,
and ultimately, our families' lives.

Our relatives are gassed, burned,
their ashes thrown in the river.
We who were selected to the right
are only temporary survivors.

Birds and butterflies never fly;
they do not like smoke in the air.
I always wished to be a bird,
so I could fly far away.

To leave this sad place,
and go home to my parents.
But I do not have wings
to fly like a bird or butterfly.

How "Canada" Was in Poland

During my stay in Auschwitz-II/Birkenau
I heard that some deportees worked in Canada.
In my mind I could not comprehend
how anyone could work in "Canada."
We were in Poland, in Central Europe.

Everyone knew that "Canada"
was overseas in North America.
Only after the Second World War
did I really understand the true meaning of
how and why "Canada" existed in Poland.

From many European countries Jews
were free prey to the Nazi terror.
Many European countries also had many
collaborators to help deport Jews.
On arrival luggage remained at the ramp.

Clothes from the disinfection building, from
the undressing entry room to the gas chambers,
were transferred to workers in "Canada."
Items were checked for hidden valuables.
Shoes and clothes were packed, then shipped to Germany.

Jews' belongings were distributed as bonuses
to loyal German citizens. Workers in "Canada"
prepared the shipments. Often I wonder,
did those clothes not have a smell of death?
Did the package recipient know their origin?

At the daily selection in Auschwitz-II/Birkenau
the selected one never knew where she would be going.
Some were assigned to sort the huge pile of clothes,
shoes, or other belongings of the deportees.
They witnessed how Jews were robbed.

Jews' belongings were taken even after death
and transported to the area called "Canada."
Those who sorted piles of stock had a chance
to get a piece of bread which some desperate
Jew had brought to this hell on earth.

The group who was selected to work in "Canada"
had the opportunity to change clothes, shoes,
get some food and other necessary hygienic items.
In Auschwitz-II/Birkenau, the disinfection building,
the four crematoriums and the unloading ramp
supplied plenty of material to the area named "Canada".

I am formerly from the Netherlands where we lived for centuries in peace and freedom! On January 13, 1944 [we were transported] in cattle cars for 3 days to Auschwitz, from there to Birkenau, and from there to Bryschinki Third Gas chamber. We worked there in the "White Effect" or as we called it "Canada," where we had to fold the clothes of people who were being gassed. We had it a little bit better [than others] because in the clothes we had to fold were sometimes dollars with which you could barter. Sometimes in the suitcases there was food, which of course, was the most important commodity. We worked in Canada from [the] end of April 1944 to January 18, 1945.

—Josephina S. Prins, Number on arm: 74934

How Was My Mother Murdered? With Gas or Bullet?

The convoy with new deportees halted. Everyone was ordered to get out. On a cart pulled by men were thrown, on top of one another, sick, old, small babies and the dead. It flashed through my mind how the sick and dead were thrown on top of one another.

My dear mother thought that we would see our neighbor from down on our street with her three girls as we did at home. Mommy thought she would leave my brother in her care while we worked. In this turmoil our neighbor was not around. We didn't know where we were.

We were deceived. Everything happened as fast as lightning. My mother was holding my brother in her arms. Poor little boy, five years old, hungry, exhausted, had no strength to walk. But he did not cry. I was next to them. Someone pushed me away, I waved and ran to catch the few others directed to the right.

My mother and brother looked in the direction my group departed. I never saw them again. The other group in which my mother and brother remained grew larger. They were standing next to the cattle car in which we had been traveling for seven days. No one with a normal mind could imagine their doomed fate.

I always see my thirty-seven year old, beautiful mother and my handsome five year old brother. I am tormented by how my dear ones were murdered.

Were they lucky to be killed in the gas chambers so my loved ones did not suffer for too long? Or as others who were dragged to the smoky pit, was Mother shot with a bullet behind her ear? Or half alive, mortally wounded, was Mommy thrown in the fire on top of other Martyrs? The young were thrown alive into fire; the sadistic horde did not waste a bullet on children.

There was no personal identification—only dead bodies. Who can tell me how my dear ones were killed? By a miracle, some of those who witnessed the massacre of European Jews survived.

Roll Call in Birkenau

We were surrounded with barbed wire. In the shadow of four smoky chimneys, all of us had roll call twice a day. It began at daybreak and lasted a few hours. Midday started the afternoon roll call and ended when the sun went to sleep. It got dark, so for that day roll call ended. Then Kapos let us go to sleep.

Our beds were large, made from raw wood, three levels on top of one another. Fourteen women slept on each level. When we moved splinters stuck our bodies. Fourteen of us had one blanket. There was no space between our tortured bodies. We were like sardines in a can. When one turned, all had to turn. We slept one head next to a pair of legs. We could smell the other person's feet. Our exhausted, weakened bodies could not take the misery for too long.

On our bodies, we had only a dress and our shoes were wooden clogs. Often it rained, so we got soaking wet; our bodies couldn't resist for too long. It did not matter that we were young. Many collapsed and some caught cold. At every roll call there were selections. The Germans took the weakened away.

Germans were helped by Kapos. They were collaborators. Kapos knew the fate of those who were selected. The ones who were selected, forever they disappeared from this hell on earth. They remained within the barbed wire. But they never had another roll call.

In Birkenau, Miri Saved My Life!

With other Jews from my hometown we were forced into box cars and locked in for seven days. We had no food, no water, not even air. On Friday, June 2, 1944, the convoy halted. We arrived at Auschwitz-II/Birkenau. The rest was like a horror dream.

Selection! I was separated from my mother and brother. Dressed in a rag, my feet in wooden clogs*, my head shaved. It rained; it was cold. It was too much for my fifteen year old body. On Sunday, June 4, 1944 during roll call, I got dizzy. It got dark. I fell on the ground.

When I opened my eyes, Miri, our Block Älteste**, poured some water on my face and said, "Child, go inside, in the block." Miri saved my life. I was not selected on that day.

(continued)

My parents in heaven watched over my fate. Miri put me to work. With a piece of brick, I scrubbed the tall chimney's brick all day. With a white bleach gel, with my fingers, I covered the cement between the brick.

In this block were over one thousand young females. Those who worked were permitted to walk; the others had to sit on the crowded three-level beds. Whoever was tall had to bend her neck and head.

There was no clean drinking water. We were hungry and thirsty. The water was yellow and rusty. It did not matter that the water was not clean, was bitter and metallic. We were thirsty. Since I worked, I was allowed to walk. Everyone said, "Kis kalyhas,*** bring water." So I carried water to the beds all day long.

Sometimes, with a group of girls, I was sent to carry large canisters with food. Close to the distribution place, in the garbage, were piles of dirty potato peels. When the Kapo looked the other way, we filled our empty stomachs with potato peels. The dirty potato peels helped me to survive.

*clogs: shoes made of wood

**Älteste is overseer appointed by the Germans. Leichner Miri was the daughter of a Rabbi from Bratislava. I have spoken with her daughter who lives in Australia.

***Kis kalyhas means little kiln. In Hungarian, it sounds very nice, but the English translation does not sound so nice

Jews from Czechoslovakia

In the summer of 1944, Jews from Theresienstadt arrived in Birkenau. They looked like ghosts. Men, women, and children were only skin and bones. Poor Jews, they were starved for years in Theresienstadt. These skeletons hardly moved; their clothes were infested; their weakened bodies could not resist for too long. Men carried away the dead daily, loaded in two rows on a cart, their stiffened naked bodies on top of one another. Men, women, and children. The dead looked like wood logs.

The few who lived a few more days ate the green bitter soup, so called food which was given to us in Lager C. Under the electrified barbed wires we pushed the bitter, dirty, green soup through to the starved Jews from Theresienstadt. We, the so-called "Hungarian Jews," could not eat the green soup. It was bitter and full of sand.

Then one day, Lager C was closed. We had to stay in our barracks and the Jews from Theresienstadt disappeared. In the Czech Lager were no more starving, dying Jews.

Daily Selection on Roll Call

At Auschwitz-II/Birkenau in Lager C, roll call was twice daily. It did not matter if it rained or was sunny. We stood five in a row for hours waiting for the SS officers to count us. We, the temporary survivors of the first selection held upon arrival in this hell, got sick and passed out on roll call. In Lager C, Nazi SS selected 100-150 young women at the morning's roll call.

One never knew who would be taken away. For us, the newcomers, it was a secret as to what happened with the selected women, but the Czech, Slovak, and Polish inmates knew their fate. Some Czech, Slovak and Polish inmates willingly helped the Nazis. Often the selected were healthy, young and beautiful. Even if we would have known their fate, we were helpless on roll call.

The SS came with rifles, barking dogs, screaming "dirty Jews." We had no water to drink, no water to wash ourselves. We were not considered humans. We were less than animals, less than flies. Nazis used healthy humans as guinea pigs. The SS forced young women into prostitution.

If one had a cold on the morning roll call she was selected; she disappeared forever. We, the most recently arrived from Hungary and territories which were invaded by the sadistic Hungarians, were named by the Czech, Slovak, and Polish inmates "grine."*

Every day I saw the tall smoky chimneys. The sky looked cloudy from the ash and smoke. I was told people worked in these factories. Years after the Second World War, I realized those factories produced only death. There innocent people were murdered, who were robbed even, after death, of their clothes, hair and any possession they might have had.

* "Grine," (pronounced greéneh,) Yiddish for the color green, was used as slang for new arrivals

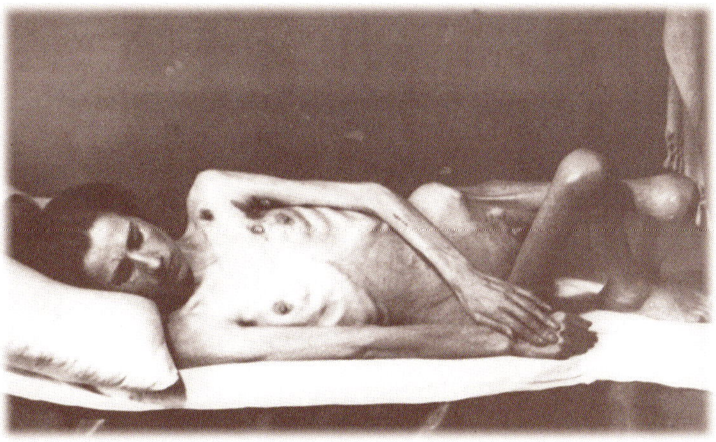

In the Shadow of Smoky Chimneys

It is always foggy and the sun never shines,
but to stay outside for hours is very hot.
It is burning hot, although the sun doesn't shine.
The greyish smoke like a blanket covers the sun.
At night the moon is covered with a foggy sky,
even though there are no clouds in the sky.
Where are the million stars from the sky?

What is in this place that the sun never shines,
the moon and every star disappear from the sky?
Why is the air so grey? Why is there so much smoke?
One can almost touch the smoky, foggy air.
There on the sandy ground in the shadow of four
chimneys, children, mothers, elderly men and women
sit on the ground. They are all hungry and thirsty.

Close by there is a faucet; the SS let everyone
have a little water. Then the group calmly waits
for its turn to enter inside to have a "sauna."
Escorting SS soldiers tell the group that after
food would be distributed. They are thirsty and hungry.
For days they dreamed of fresh air, water and food.
The group is anxious for their turn in the "sauna."

The air is foggy, but at least it is an open area.
If one would tell the truth about the "sauna"
peaceful Jews wouldn't believe they are deceived,
that those who enter the building will be gassed
and burned. If one would say, "Jew you are deceived,"
no one would believe that heavy smell of burned rubber
is their brethren who entered prior into the "sauna."

The group which arrived earlier already was gassed.
Deceived, murdered Jews' burning bodies grey the sky.
As the undressing hall to the gas chamber swallows a group,
it makes room for the next group to be gassed, murdered.

Then a car arrives with a Red Cross painted on.
It brings Cyclon B* gas which kills the new group.
Without stop the same pattern repeats day and night.

The constant arrival brings more and more deportees, innocent Jews carrying children, mothers, the old and the young. Their gassed, burned bodies will smoke and darken the sky. The factory of death works with no stop, day and night. Deceived people enter the "sauna" to clean themselves, but only their ashes remain. Continuous new transports bring European Jews day and night.

*Cyclon B (Zyklon B): crystalline hydrogen cyanide used in gas chambers

We Were Naked

There was a selection on the last day of August 1944 in Auschwitz-II/Birkenau. It was conducted by Dr. Joseph Mengele, the "famous angel of death," who used humans as guinea pigs for all kinds of experiments. From Block 18 we were ordered naked to exit through the back door and enter into Block 16 at the back entrance.

On the road armed soldiers with dogs and club sticks were assisted by Kapos who watched that no one should escape the selection. From Block 16 we exited at the front door.

There was Dr. Mengele. With his gloves he pointed some of us to the right, others to the left. My tummy was blown up from the potato peels I ate with dirt and sand from the garbage dump. Dr. Mengele pointed to me, and Vera his assistant asked, "Are you pregnant?" I did not understand her. I answered, "I am fifteen years old." Dr. Mengele waved his gloves, so I passed his selection into the larger group. Years after I realized how close, as a child, I was to my last day.

Again Dr. Mengele separated sisters, mothers. They screamed, cried and they were brutally beaten. The group on the left remained between the Blocks. We were naked, trying to warm one another. None of us witnessed it, but through history it is known that those selected to the left side were transported and murdered on that day.

Our group was ushered to the disinfection building. After the bath we got other rags on our bodies, wooden clogs, but no undergarments. As our group got close to the ramp we were ordered to return.

The female officers escorted us into another lager. There the fence was covered with blankets. Behind the fence smoke rose from the ground. Occasionally high red smoky flames erupted. The strong smell of burned rubber was intense.

We were ordered to undress in the open yard. Our large group from Lager C stayed naked outside. The next day we were ordered to get inside the Block.

The rooms were small and the floor paved with wood. Pajama tops and warm liquid was distributed. By bad luck I got pajama pants. The distributor got angry, and she gave me a punch which broke one of my teeth. My heart was so bitter that I did not feel the pain.

Sketch by Author

Misery Changes Human Behavior Some Detainees' Lives Improve

In concentration camps life was miserable. Those in forced labor camps were beaten and most of them were kept in the open fields. For the prisoners of war, life was somehow better. It was more bearable than for those detained in camps. Most detainees suffered hunger, infestation, beatings and cold, which decimated everyone.

Human feeling disappeared for the majority of inmates who were incarcerated for many years. They willingly collaborated with the Nazis. I think those who helped the SS Germans were given drugs to behave so inhumanely toward us. They brutalized, tortured and beat the new detainees to death. Their title was "Kapo.*" They had no human feelings towards humanity.

Jewish detainees were treated with more brutality than Gentiles of any other nationality. As an example, before sunrise each morning, rain or shine, Kapos screamed and beat detainees of three blocks**, ordering them to run into the wash trailer. (I try to write how it was.) In every block there were about 1200 women, yet detainees from three barracks squeezed into one wash trailer. In twenty minutes we had to wash our face and use the latrine. There was no soap, towel, paper, or enough space to stand next to one another. Then we ran to stand for roll call.

In a few months, upon a selection, I was shipped with a large group into a factory in Fallersleben, Germany. Here it was better. We had warm water to wash ourselves, a single bunk bed with one blanket, a straw mattress, a straw pillow, and a semi-heated room with some lights. Compared to Auschwitz-II/Birkenau this was a big change in our lifestyle, but we still had wooden shoes, one rag on our back, no undergarment or change of clothes.

Each morning and evening I ran to take a shower. The lukewarm water refreshed my tired body. We also had a toilet, but no papers or towels to wipe or clean ourselves.

Female officers counted, then escorted us across the road to work. From the factory entrance we walked deep down to a lower level and entered into a large room with large machines. Six of us were put to work in a narrow hallway. Above, there was a grate where people walked.

* Kapo: an overseer appointed by the Germans
** block: a large trailer

A German Meister Brought Me Salt

From Auschwitz-II/Birkenau our group of five hundred arrived in Fallersleben. The next day about half of us were escorted into the factory. We six were selected to work in the painting department. It was a narrow hallway. The material to be painted entered on an assembly chain. It was a heavy round metal object with a handle. The oval top on its center had a six angle screw with a diameter of seven and depth of two centimeters. It looked like a flower. On one side there was a small hole where no paint was allowed. If paint accidentally leaked into the hole one of the three meisters* complained to the female SS officers, who screamed at us. The paint was in large containers. Rubber hoses were hooked to them. With one hand we pressed a pistol to spray paint and with the other turned a rotating tray attached to the table. The finished objects were hooked on the assembly chain which rolled into the dryer room.

We worked for twelve hours a day. My arms and back hurt. In front of us there was a large ventilator. Above was a grate where people walked. We were given a mask, working gloves, a short jacket, and a half liter skimmed milk.

In October 1944 my mouth bled. It leaked on my chin, and I had nothing to wipe the blood. Our German meister, a kind gentlemen, risked his freedom and brought a handful of salt. He said, "Little child, rinse your mouth twice daily with the salt." The bleeding stopped, but I got a gum disease. The gums shrank and the roots were exposed. It was painful. Later, at the age of twenty my lower teeth were pulled, also most of the upper. Since the gum shrinks, I often must replace the removable teeth. It is unpleasant and costly.

In December of 1944, I began to cough and choke on big lumps of paint. I had terrible pain in my back. Shivering with fever, I asked not to be sent to work. Our medical person was a dental technician. She roughly said, "Elly, you must go to work." Tears came into my eyes. It ran through my mind that when I go home, I will tell my parents that she was not nice toward me.

With the blanket on my back I walked out from her office and the Hauptscharführer** with a club in his hand entered. A few girls were in the hallway. They curiously looked on. Another miracle happened. The high ranking officer asked, "Are you sick little child?" Prior, if one was caught with a blanket on her back she was beaten. The sick were sent away. They disappeared. He called the Lager Älteste*** Heller Brana and said to her, "Put Elly to wash floors in the living quarters." From then on I was not exposed to additional factory fumes.

*Meister: instructor for work performance **Hauptscharführer high ranking officer
***Lager Älteste: appointee who assigned work

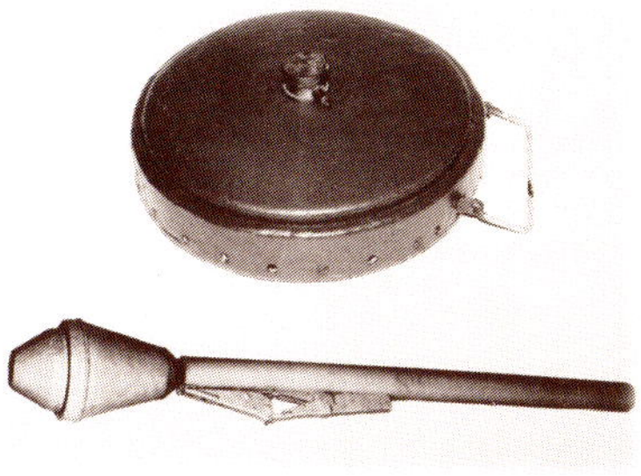

My First Craft in Fallersleben

In Fallersleben everyone got a cup and bowl, her own spoon too. The turnip soup was distributed hot. We had a single bed with a straw mattress. It was such a change after Auschwitz-II/Birkenau. The living standard and food could not be compared to those in the concentration camp of Auschwitz-II/Birkenau. There we slept like sardines, and the food was a bitter green soup with sand. There were long hours of roll call in the rain and in the sun.

(continued)

In Fallersleben we had a semi-heated room, inside toilet, but we did not have toilet paper. We had a shower with lukewarm water morning and evening. To dry ourselves, there were no towels. Our bodies dried fast. Then we stood in line for food.

Since I worked in the painting department I had access to black and beige paint. I painted on the cup and bowl my name, flowers, and other designs. Our female overseer, Anna-Marie, observed. She was a pretty blonde female officer who often counted and escorted us to work. The factory was across from our living quarters. With a smile Anna-Marie said, "Elly come here." I was terrified, ready for a blow to my body. I was seldom punished, but I did witness others when they were beaten. By not asking permission to paint my accessories, I was guilty.

Anna-Marie smiled. I closed my eyes, ready to be beaten with her ever present club. She said, "Elly, paint a design on my cup." Anna-Marie liked her name and the flowers I painted on her cup.

The next day she gave me a green sweater, white thread and needle. She said, "Elly, sew designs on my sweater." The German officer Anna-Marie liked the design on her sweater, but I did not get a reward or extra privilege for my work. I was a slave. I continued to work in the factory, but it gave me great satisfaction that I created something.

The Factory Complex

In Fallersleben, Germany, the Volkswagen factory was in a large rectangular area. As I recall, the complex had many individual buildings. Both ends were connected like a bridge, from end to end. Under the bridge of each building, like on a highway, trucks carried material and people in the factory. On an assembly chain and on gigantic cranes, production parts were transported from one end of a building to the other end.

The factory complex was connected. Large trucks arrived daily and carried the finished production, also the needed materials to each building and to the harbor. On the channel, vessels were loaded and unloaded. The Volkswagen auto factory built a tremendous complex. During the War it changed its production and workers.

From Auschwitz-II/Birkenau, my group of five hundred arrived at the Volkswagen factory in Fallersleben on September 3, 1944. In one of the factory buildings we were housed on the main floor. Soldiers escorted us daily to work and back. In the section of the factory complex where I worked, no auto parts were made. I had a chance to see how gigantic the Volkswagen complex was.

(continued)

We five girls were escorted by a female soldier, Christine, to a nearby men's lager in Laadberg. We crossed a bridge. On shore we walked forward. Laadberg's camp was surrounded with barbed wire. In Laadberg we altered garments for Hauptscharführer Hanz Johanes Pump. It was winter, January 1945. Our bodies were covered with rags; on our feet we had wooden clogs. We did not have undergarments, jackets or socks. The fresh air cleaned our lungs. It was cold. The ground was powdered with freshly fallen white snow.

Once, in the sky, planes appeared. They looked like silver birds. Soldier Christine ordered us to walk fast, to return to the bunker. Often there were air raids. The factory did not stop its production during air raids. In the living quarters it did not matter if it was day or night. We were ordered into the bunker as many as four to five times day and night. Due to lack of sleep some factory workers were injured.

Please Come Mommy. I Miss You.

Mommy all my teeth hurt and
my mouth is always bleeding.
I am cold. Where are you Mommy?
I miss you. Please come Mommy.
Put your hand around my shoulder,
kiss my cheek, my dear mother.
I am alone among strangers.

As soon I see you dear Mommy
all my pain will go away.
My back hurts. I am cold
and shivering. Come to me Mommy.
Surrounded by strangers,
no one cares that I am alone.
I miss you. Please come Mommy.

Mommy, I have a fever, I am cold.
Come to see me for a day or two.
Put your hand on my forehead,
so the fever and pain will go away.
I ask adults, "Where is my mommy?
Please tell my mommy I miss her."
No one tells me where my mommy is.

Adults do not help or ask how I feel.
I have a sharp pain in my back Mommy.
I cough badly and I am ready to choke
on large lumps of stinky beige paint.
Come put your hand on my shoulder,
so I will stop coughing beige paint.
Each day I pray that you come to see me Mommy.

Mommy I miss your hug, your kindness
and your love. Come to your daughter.
Please put your hand on my back
and forehead, so the pain will go away.
As soon I see your lovely face,
feel your kiss and touch on my forehead,
all my sickness will go away.

Dear Mommy, when will you come to see me?
I am coughing loudly; it disturbs everyone
and they complain. No one can sleep.
I am fifteen, a child. Please come Mommy.
Help your daughter to get better. Put your
hand on my forehead, on my back, so all
my sickness will go away. I miss you Mommy.

Allied Soldiers Rolled In

Anxiously, I was counting the days, even though I seldom knew the date or the days of the week. It did not matter rain or shine. Twice a day in rags we stayed on roll call for many hours waiting for the SS soldiers to count. Daily soldiers selected some girls and took them away. We newcomers never knew the fate of the selected ones.

The heavy smoke in the air made the sky grey. At night new transports arrived. I heard children cry. There were days, some ran screaming into the barbed wires. They turned dark grey and died instantly. Every day I thought one day the misery would end and I could go home to tell my parents what I witnessed. Our days in this camp were like hell on earth.

Often I thought, “Life is not fair.” First, my father was taken away from us, then the Ghetto, then deportation, squeezed into cattle cars. On arrival, the selection to this hell on earth. Separation from my mother and brother. Later shipment with a group of strangers to Fallersleben to work in a factory.

I was only fifteen years old and got sick. Daily there were air raids, and SS soldiers took us in the bunker. Beginning of April 1945 female soldiers escorted our group to the railroad and ordered us in cattle cars. The train rolled, then halted. SS soldiers ushered us with rifles and dogs in a lager surrounded with barbed wire.

We entered into the yard and met a group of girls. They were part of the large group selected at the end of August 1944 in Auschwitz-II/Birkenau. They were shipped to this place, Salzwedel. My group was transported to Fallersleben. As we mingled, some family members were reunited. With us, the newcomers, food shortage doubled.

Then suddenly SS German soldiers disappeared. On April 14, 1945 the sun began to shine bright as Allied and American soldiers rolled through the gate, and they said, "You girls are free." I didn't comprehend the word "free," but other girls did. They sang and danced and said "We will go home." That I understood. "Home to my family. Yes! There I want to go."

Three Cousins Reunited

The death gate is the entrance to Birkenau. Above the gate there is a spiral staircase leading to a room with windows. On the horizon as far as one can see is a huge wasteland of 172 hectares, with remnants of chimneys. Every two are connected with a brick pipe.

On Friday June 2, 1944 our transport arrived in Birkenau, during the peak liquidation of Hungarian Jews and Jews from countries which had been invaded by Hungary. On arrival I noticed a foggy sky and smoke in the air. The selection began quickly. The sick were thrown on a cart. Young to the right; mothers, children and old to the left. My group was directed to the right.

Our clothes were taken, our heads shaven, and we were pushed into hot and cold showers. We got a rag on our back, wooden clogs on our feet and were ordered to walk. Our group walked between sections surrounded with barbed wire. Lager C was a section with thirty-two wooden barracks. Each barrack housed 1000-1200 females. They sat on three levels of beds. We, from the region Salaj, were housed in the Block 20. It was cold and a rainy day.

Mud and fifty centimeters of water were inside. The next morning a miracle happened. My name was called. From Block 18 the Block Älteste, Leichner Miri, arrived with a small group of females, but I did not recognize who called my name. There, with shaved heads and dressed in rags, were my two cousins from the region Bihor.

I was transferred to Block 18 where my cousins were. They had arrived two weeks earlier. We slept like sardines in a can. Fourteen on a raw wood bed with splinters; to cover ourselves we shared one blanket. Lager C was very crowded. Twice daily during roll calls SS soldiers, assisted by Kapos, selected 100-150 young women. We new arrivals did not know where they were taken. They disappeared and no one ever saw them again.

In a few months, a large group of few a thousand was selected. We were shipped from Auschwitz-II/Birkenau to Germany to work as slaves in various factories. I was separated from my two cousins. I worked in Fallersleben. As the Allies got closer, our group was evacuated to Salzwedel. I was reunited with my two cousins again.

On April 14, 1945 the Lager was liberated by the American Army. The three of us survived with broken hearts. The misery we lived through forever haunts us. We lost our parents, brothers, sisters, aunts, uncles, cousins, grandmothers and friends. They were all massacred. Our parents' homes were ransacked.

We will never forget our loss. Our life circle sent us in different directions. Then unexpectedly by fate, the three cousins, Violet, Eva, and I, again were reunited in New York City.

Collage by Author:
Eva, Violet and Elly
New York,1971

Klari (Andrew's girlfriend),
Eva, Andrew (mother's cousin),
Elly, Violet
Hillersleben, Germany,
July 25, 1945

We Got Our Freedom and Ran Away

The American and Allied army made us free on April 14, 1945. With others we were free to go anywhere we wished. But how? No money, no parents or guardian to direct our steps. How to get home from Germany into my country and hometown, to my parents and brother. I am in Salzwedel, far away from my family. Americans with the Allies gave us freedom. We are not slaves. But what is the next step? In infested wooden barracks we were in a camp. The Allies first loaded us girls on open trucks and moved everyone in to the Salzwedel armory. They placed five girls in a room with single beds. We could walk and sleep when or where we wanted.

The armory was in a large area surrounded by trees, green fields and many benches. Once a day food was distributed, food for everyone. Someone gave my cousin two large raw potatoes. With a shard of metal she scrubbed, then rinsed those potatoes and put them in a bowl to prepare a fresh meal for us. I collected some dry branches and leaves for the fire. We found two bricks, placed them close to one another and then rubbed two stones until they sparked. A small fire started between the two bricks. The aroma of boiling potato filled the area.

Suddenly a Jeep stopped and two uniformed soldiers walked out. They brought a can of meat, opened it, and poured it on our potatoes. They put a whole can of meat on our potatoes! We were shocked! The can would have been enough for two more times. One of the soldiers brought two spoons and sat close to us on the ground. They were smiling ear to ear and talking, but we did not understand what they said. We did not speak their language, English.

The three of us got scared. We ran away and left our food, the potato with meat, in the yard. We were hiding in the closet and under the bed. The two soldiers looked for us in every room. Probably they wished to explain the situation. They wanted to feed us with some good food. This is the way we celebrated our freedom. We ran away.

I Lived Through Heartbreaking Truth

I arrived in my hometown with high hope and thought how good it is to get home. To see my parents and brother in our home. From the train station I ran through the streets. Strangers lived in the house. There, no one seemed to know the whereabouts of my parents.

Later a man said, "Your mother was murdered on arrival in Auschwitz-II/Birkenau." Another man who was drafted with Daddy into a forced labor camp said, "Your father was burned alive in the spring of 1943." Oh no, no! Life cannot be so cruel. Both men must not be telling me the truth.

The ground moved under my feet. I lost my voice, my smile, my hope. In my dream Mommy said, "Do not worry. My two brothers in South America will take you into their home." I wrote my uncles, "What should I do?" An answer to my letter never arrived. In my dream, I asked Daddy's advice. He said, "My three brothers live in South America. One of them will take you into his home." I asked them, "What should I do?" The three brothers never wrote an answer. Five uncles could not take care of me. I did not know what to do, where to go.

City officials moved the people who lived in my parents' house. In the ransacked empty home, in my hometown, I walked like a zombie. My parents in heaven prayed for my well-being. I met my future husband. Slowly I began to talk, but I think of my parents and brother with sorrow, and I am bitter about the painful past.

Long ago I forgave my parents' five brothers* who left an orphan child to suffer alone. The loss of everything that is dear to anyone: my parents, my brother, my other relatives, and the security of having a home. At the age of fifteen I remained alone, facing the heartbreaking cruel truth.

*My parents' five brothers, I wished to be as real uncles; they were not.

Homecoming

After the Second World War, a few Jews returned with broken hearts. They were not welcomed by the locals. Many families had no survivors. Still the Hungarians asked, "Why were not all Jews killed?"

The city people were void of sympathy, looted belongings, and seized properties that were not returned to their owners. The surviving orphans were threatened by Hungarians.

In the sky, the sun shone bright; at night the sky had stars and the moon gave light. But for the few Jews who survived in extreme anguish, it remained forever dark, a frightful nightmare.

Jewish orphans returned from the hell with bitter hearts. They left the city to begin a new life, but they never forget the pain of the dark misery they lived through.

My homecoming was the same as that of many other orphans.* I left the lonely, empty house, the unfriendly locals and my hometown. Then I struggled to stand on my shaky, trembling feet.

*Afraid of my own shadow, as a child with hope, I returned home. I hid in the shed where my parents had kept wood for heating. The tenant, who lived in part of the house, yelled at me. With nothing at home for me, I left my parents' house and never went back. Many years later, the house was given to a Hungarian couple.

Survival with a Broken Heart

I eagerly looked forward to seeing my parents. With emotion I arrived in my hometown. From the train station, I ran on the city's gradually elevating streets. To be home, to get a hug from my parents! To see my brother and return to school. I had so much hope for the future.

At my parents' house, in our apartment, a large family of strangers lived. The next day city officials relocated them. The rigid empty rooms scared me. I did not have a bucket to bring water from the well or a glass from which to drink. I had no one to give me food to eat. Bitterly, I sat on the dirty wooden floor.

Then I was invited to my parents' tenants', for a plate of soup and a bed to sleep. On the cover's corner my name was embroidered. Like turning on a light, it hit my memory. When I was eight years old Mommy made the cover. I asked, "This is the cover Mommy made for me?" She said, "No, I embroidered your name on it."

The same thing happened at my best friend's home. Years ago the two mothers were good friends. It seemed so long ago; maybe it was just a dream. One night I was invited there for dinner and to sleep. The pillow case and the quilt cover were light pink, imprinted with small white flowers and leaves.

Years ago a girl was given a dowry. Parents began early buying for their child. My parents bought the pink material for me. Mommy trusted her friend and gave it to her for safekeeping because everything was confiscated from Jews by the Hungarian law. I asked, "This is the material Mommy brought here?" She said, "Your mother never gave me anything."I could not force her to return the material. Anyway, it was already sewn into pillow cases and quilt covers.

The wind blew away my dreams to be with my family. Heartbroken, I survived alone.

The Rooster Is Calling "Good Morning!"

In my childhood memory there is a popular song which promises hope for Jews: The rooster calls daily, "Good morning, Messiah soon will arrive. The Messiah's legs are green and his wings are shiny gold." The song ends with the question, "But when will the Messiah come?" In the rooster's song is a promise: Messiah will come to save every Jew. But for an unknown reason He did not arrive.

The globe closed its heart and eyes. Very few cared about the fate of forgotten Jews. The sadistic hordes of many European nations, with zeal, helped Nazis to murder Jews. Upon our misery, the collaborators had fun torturing us. Laughing, they said to Jews, "Messiah didn't come to save you, dirty Jew!"

Our parents awaited the Messiah, but He did not arrive to save millions of our brethren as they were gassed in the crematoria of Birkenau. Their bodies were burned in the ovens and their ashes used as fertilizer.

In the summer of 1944, the arrival of new deportees took on a new scale. The ovens did not have the capacity to burn the massacred bodies. In the adjoining forest a huge, deep ditch for the gassed bodies was dug. They were thrown in the ditch and burned. After a half century, the ditch was filled with water, so there is a huge, deep lake.* But the water in this lake is black.

Religious leaders for years have brought bags of white sand from the Holy Land. They tried to clear the water in the lake. Although for many years white sand was thrown in the lake, the water does not clear; it remains black. Around the lake there are a few trees. But in the water not even a fly lives.

*I visited the lake April 13, 1999.

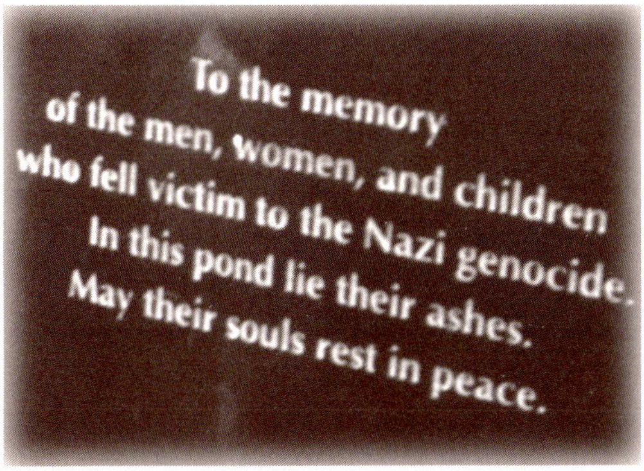

Memories Which Still Do Not Fade

My parents. My brother. Family members. My lost home. Other bad childhood memories. As I age the memories reappear like a twilight horror movie.

Two years had passed since my Father was taken from my life. Then with Mommy and my little brother we were forced out from our home, forced in a ghetto, and a few weeks later herded and locked into a cattle car with more than ninety-five strangers. The memory from inside the closed box car. A newborn baby's first cry. The cry when someone's family member just died and was rolled into a corner.

The memory of the relief as the locked door was opened and we were ordered out from the box car. The selection when my mother and brother faded forever from my sight, from my life. A deep scar was left on my heart. These memories never fade: the crying new born, the new mother, the sick and the dead thrown on top of one another on a cart pulled by men who wore striped rags, their faces ashen grey.

(continued)

The morning and evening roll call in Lager C lasted for hours. It did not matter that it often rained. Memories of the dirt road with sand and stone, the grey smoky sky, the invisible hot sun. I lost the sense of the day of the week and the time of the day, but the memory of screaming young women, as they ran into the barbed wires and their bodies turned grey as they died, is still with me.

The adult's answer to my question as to the whereabouts of my mother was, "Do not worry. She is with your brother in a warmer climate." How was I so stupid or naïve a child that I could have believed the lie? Did that adult know my loved ones' fate? Why had she lied to a child? Maybe she knew the truth that the continuous smoke in the air was from our loved ones' burning bodies.

The wish to see my family kept me alive. I would have not survived knowing the truth. The cruel memories do not fade.

My Husband's Story

Ernest, age 21, drafted to forced labor in 1942.

This is a true story about my husband's youth and others who were born in Europe, especially in Hungary and parts of other countries which were invaded by Huns. In 1942 the Hungarian government drafted Jews between the ages of eighteen to fifty-five. Ernest was twenty-one years old. Young men were forced to work hard labor.

They were beaten. Without food or warm clothes, they slept outside in the frozen snow. During the cold nights some froze to death. From the original group over 90% died. They were forced on foot to walk to Polish lands and into the Russian tundra. At the end of 1943 the Hungarian/German Allies were pushed back from Poland and Russia.

The handful of the young men on foot were forced by armed soldiers to retreat to Hungary. Those who were still alive were placed in a shed in the city of Balf, at the Austria-Hungary border. They had typhus and high fevers for days. My husband lost consciousness. When he awoke he crawled from the place he had been lying for some time.

He remembers, "I rolled a stick on the blanket; the lice on it were as thick as the blanket. In a few days we were forced to walk again. Those who could not walk were shot on the spot." In history this is known as "The Death March." He continued, "Few survivors got to Austria's Dachau, Mauthausen, Gunskichen and Wels."

The skeleton-like survivors were liberated by Allied Forces on May 6, 1945. Slowly they went home. There were no family members, just empty homes. Every household belonging had been ransacked. The handful of survivors worked hard. They tried to put their broken lives together. The young married and raised families. Each survivor was marked by that hard time.

This is not fiction. This happened in my husband's youth.

The Author married Ernest Gross on June 24,1946.

The Oppressed Revolted

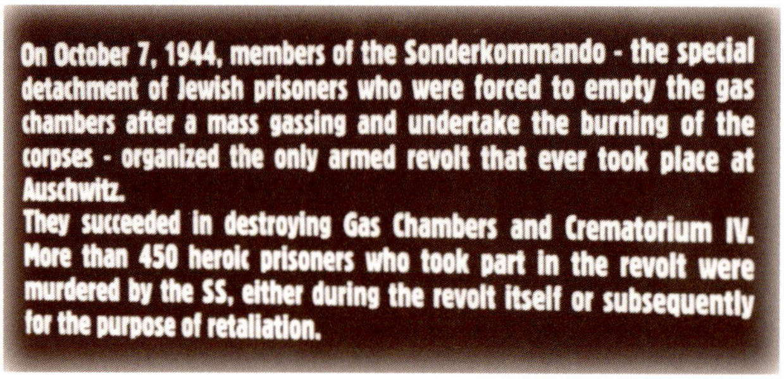

On October 7, 1944, members of the Sonderkommando—the special detachment of Jewish prisoners who were forced to empty the gas chambers after a mass gassing and undertake the burning of the corpses-organized the only armed revolt that ever took place at Auschwitz. They succeeded in destroying Gas Chambers and Crematorium IV. More than 450 heroic prisoners who took part in the revolt were murdered by the SS, either during the revolt itself or subsequently for the purpose of retaliation.

In my childhood I always heard that Jews never revolted. Even my Mother told me when someone says something you don't like, try to walk away without saying anything. Jews were oppressed by every nation in the world. The revolt was not my accomplishment; I was not there to contribute to the revolt. But I am very proud to read about it and retell the story of the Auschwitz-II/Birkenau detainees who worked in the gas chambers and crematorium and revolted.

Sonderkommando was the name of the group of men who worked in the crematorium. Their job was gruesome. Many did not wish to live and took sleeping pills to die. Their life was the most miserable work anyone could imagine. Every few months the Nazis killed the group who worked there and replaced them with a group from the new arrivals.

Then one day, with the help of seven young, brave women, dynamite was smuggled in the Crematorium #4. The brave men who worked as the Sonderkommando blew up Crematorium #4. It is history. We must remember they were unimaginably brave.

After the revolt, Nazi soldiers murdered every man. This heroic revolt was in the autumn of 1944. The group of young women who smuggled the dynamite and the Sonderkommando men who made the explosion are among the most heroic people in our history. Of the seven women who smuggled the dynamite into the crematorium, by a twist of fate, two sisters survived. Crematorium #4 was destroyed beyond repair.

In Auschwitz-I there still stands a small gas chamber. Auschwitz-II/Birkenau had four large gas chambers and crematoriums. Each gas chamber had the capacity to kill about three thousand deceived innocents in twenty minutes. In European countries, Jews were made almost extinct in the factories of death. Why were four gigantic gas chambers and crematoriums needed? Who would have been the Nazi regime's next victim?

Letter to My Mother

Although many years have passed since we have seen each other, my dear mother, I always see your beautiful face and smile. I feel your love for your two children. Father was drafted into forced labor, and you Mother were struggling very hard to make ends meet. Around the world, a mother like you would have deserved a Nobel Prize.

The last time we spoke was on a Friday. It was June 2, 1944. Upon our arrival to Auschwitz-II/Birkenau, during that turmoil you, Mommy, asked me, "Should I give your brother

(continued)

to the care of our neighbor?" You continued, "She has three children between the ages one and four." I answered, "I am fifteen and Brother is five years old. I can take care of myself better than a little boy." It took less than a minute.

With a wave of the hand, I was pushed to the right, and we did not see each other again. Because of my love for my little brother and you, my dear mother, you were gassed, and you were only thirty-seven years old.

My poor little brother died in your arms. He was not a lonely frightened child. The two of you entered into heaven. I hope you met Daddy in heaven, and the three of you are waiting for me.

You, Mommy, died not knowing that the Hungarians murdered Daddy in the spring of 1943, on the Russian front. The Hungarian government did not notify our family of Father's death. Daddy doesn't have a gravesite, nor you Mommy, nor my brother.

To honor the tragic past, with a large group of teenagers, I have visited Auschwitz-II/Birkenau a few times. The famous Black Lake and the crematorium ruins are the only gravesite.

The Little Lonely Child

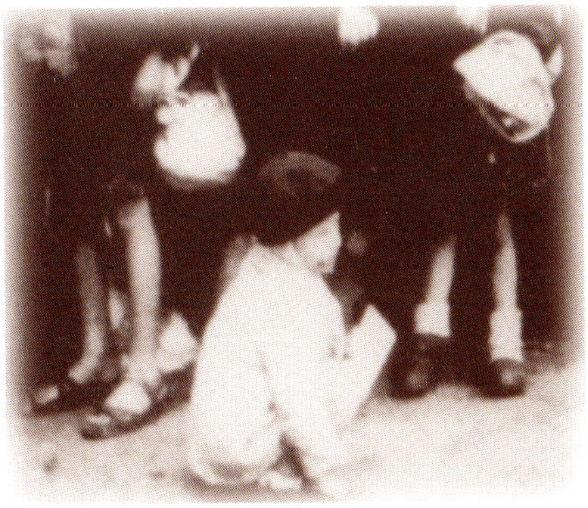

In the center of this photo, a little child sits alone. On the road he sits by himself. Perhaps his siblings were directed to the right, so he remained alone. Poor little lonely, hungry boy. He sits like a little puppy. He is waiting for his relatives. Maybe his mother or grandmother, or the person in whose care he was left. In this mad world he is a lost little boy who is scared and forgotten by everyone.

In the photo are other children and adults who are condemned to die in the gas chambers of Birkenau. By the Nazi standards they have no value. They are young mothers with young children. Why in the world did no one care that this happened? Why were all these beautiful young mothers and children murdered? Their only crime is that they were born Jewish, so by the SS and collaborators they must die. On the entire globe has everyone gone mad? Every nation closes its eyes and ears. No one wants to hear the Jewish people cry.

When SS soldiers, with barking dogs and rifles ready to shoot, order the group to move, I can imagine the little frightened boy. He does not understand the command. Perhaps a Nazi soldier kicks him with his boots. The poor little boy does not understand why everything has changed around him. Why was he left alone? No one kisses him; no one hugs him; no one feeds him. In the center he is waiting for his siblings. Maybe the Nazi soldier throws him on a cart pulled by men, on top or between the old, sick and dead. Maybe he was pushed into the gas chamber. Hopefully he did not suffer long.

In Memory of Our Martyrs

For years, in the news untold stories began to be written. Aged witnesses testified about the Holocaust. Readers acquired knowledge of those who were massacred and those who survived. Some survivors were silent for over fifty years. Yet, some had the courage to talk and tell the horror they lived through, so the next generation would remember our Martyrs.

I'm sorry that I agreed to talk, but my mother would say, "You my child, must tell others not to forget what happened to us." My mother would say, "If you are silent, others will never know." My mother would continue, "How hard we worked and how peaceful we were. G'd will give you strength to tell others how we lived, and how we were murdered. You, my child, must remember the dark years of our history. Your generation is the last who survived. Remind others to tell their story to their children, to the next generation."

In the memory of our families who were brutally murdered, we who are still alive have an obligation. It is our duty to share our memories with others. If we remain silent, it is as if we murder them again.

Let people read and hear from the witnesses.

(Not) Every Life Returns in Birkenau

A snail slowly crawls on the grassy ground in Birkenau. The snail is not afraid to crawl. She can have a feast on the grass. But over a half century ago a snail did not crawl in Birkenau. The snail would have been a feast to the hungry starving inmates. On the grassy ground there are frogs and bugs jumping. Half a century ago nature was dead. There was no grass on the ground.

Every spring, nature renews itself; life begins. Butterflies and birds fly in the clear sky. Snails crawl, frogs and bugs jump. The snail crawls on the top of the blown-up crematorium. Butterflies and birds fly over the camp's remnants. Yearly, young Jewish children come to visit Birkenau. They witness the cemetery where there are no gravestones. From around the globe Jews come to say Kaddish* in Birkenau. In Birkenau millions of Jews were tortured, gassed and burned, their ashes used to fertilize these huge killing fields.

Snails, frogs, bugs, birds and butterflies renew life each year in Birkenau. They can have a feast on the grassy ground. The inmates' lives were cut short and they can never return.

We Jews come from many parts of the world to ease our pain. We light candles in memory of our families, our martyrs, and with sorrow we leave Birkenau.

*Kaddish: Jewish hymn in praise of G'd; mourner's prayer for the dead

The Grass is Green

Now in Birkenau the grass is green. Each little blade of grass grows on our families' blood and we step on the green grass. While we walk on the grass we do not think that the grass grows on the ashes of our relatives. If the grass could talk it would say to us, "Do not step on me, because I am green grass and I grow from someone's ashes."

In the years of 1940-1945, grass did not grow in Auschwitz-II/Birkenau. There was only sand and stone and always freezing rain. The rain chilled our bones. We did not have warm clothes. Even inside in the wooden barracks, it was always cold. In the 1940's German soldiers, with barking dogs and rifles ready to shoot, made sure no one escaped the crematoria's gas chambers.

To us who lived through the terror of the concentration camps, to our aching hearts, the change we witness brings great feeling. We did not think that one day the time would come that we could walk freely from Auschwitz to Birkenau on the guarded road.

Now, Polish police watch with care that none of us should get hurt. The change in history is great, even though we step on blood-stained grass.

The Long Row of Blue Jackets

At the sound of the shofar* I become very emotional that we Jews can freely walk on the paved road. From the Auschwitz main camp I walk to Auschwitz-II/Birkenau. On the three kilometer road, I walk with my fellow marchers. We are a large group of teenagers and a few survivors. We survivors age quickly. We won't walk for too long.

The trip to Poland is tiring, very emotional, and heart-wrenching. It gives me strength to see the large group of teenagers. They come from many countries; I am proud to walk with them. It eases my pain that I can share my bitter experiences. I tell these lovely Jewish teenagers my past history. Now they can tell their grandchildren the Jews' history. They can say they heard it from me and other survivors.

We walk from Auschwitz to Birkenau quietly. The young try to help the old. All of us wear blue jackets. It is heartwarming to see long rows of blue jackets. Proudly I wear my blue jacket. When we reached the small hill, there is a bridge with a small curb. I look around. There were only blue jackets.

What revenge we give to the past killers. We are a nation. We are here. We are stronger. We Jews survived against all odds.

*Shofar: ram's horn, blown during the High Holidays. The liturgy instructing Jews to hear the call of the shofar is followed by a blessing that G'd has permitted us to reach this day.

My Heart Aches

The Hungarians were eager to solve what they called "the Jewish problem." They wanted to get a free hand looting every Jewish home. From Hungary we Jews were shipped with great speed, about a half million in a month.

In Birkenau the four crematoriums could not burn our loved ones. The murderers threw our gassed brethren to burn in a deep ditch. I feel my dear mother and brother were thrown into that ditch. My heart hurts and always aches.

When I accidentally cut or hit myself, a sharp pain follows, an injury which in time eventually heals and doesn't leave a lasting mark. But my heartache is a constant shadow in my life day and night. To ease my pain I participated in the March of the Living* with teenagers a few times.

I wish to forget the history of my past and the nightmares I constantly have. They follow me when I am awake during the day and will follow me to my grave. In my dream I see the Ash Pond's black water in Birkenau and my heart beats fast. It is pumping so strong that it hurts, as if it is ready to jump out of my chest.

In my dream I see my mother floating on that water, holding my brother in her arms. She smiles beautifully, and they are both waving at me. I hear them say, "Do not follow us."

*March of the Living: a program to teach Jewish history to Jewish youth through a two week trip to Poland and Israel. Survivors and teenagers participate.

Our Daughter

When she was born,
I put a red bow in
her long auburn hair.
She had a round face
and beautiful blue eyes.

When she did not cry
I would think that
she was a doll
from a store or a
display in a museum.

When she was nine
months old she walked
and she balanced
her fragile body
with her small hands.

She was pretty, smart,
and always asked questions.
Why are leaves green?
Why does water have no color?
Why is the milk white?

Her questions never stopped.
At the age of four,
she read tales from books.
When she was five, she attended
the first year of school.

She remembered every book
she read without
looking into the book.
She was born witty
and very pretty.

(continued)

While I walked with her
people stopped to look
at her beautiful face.
I was proud to have
such a pretty child.

She grew to be
a successful woman,
a wife, the mother of two,
and remains a loving,
pretty daughter to us.

Chibi, the Little Chick!

Mother Hen has nineteen chicks. They are covered with yellow puffs. Some chicks have puffy dark spots. The chicks are always hungry and they are always cold. The little chicks are hiding under Mother's wings and tummy. She keeps them warm. Nineteen chicks are too many and it is crowded under Mother Hen.

To get under Mother's protection, the stronger chick pushes out the weak ones. Mother Hen cannot protect them all at once, so she must move right and left to warm them all.

With her constant moving, an accident occurs. She steps on a chick's leg. Mother Hen accidently breaks a little chick's fragile leg. Our son is five years old and he runs to help the injured chick. He prepares matches with a string. The boy puts a cast on the chick's leg, To keep it warm, he puts it under his shirt. He places the chick in a large basket, and he often feeds the little chick. He names the puffy chick "Chibi." And when he leaves for kindergarten he makes sure the chick is warm and fed.

"Chibi" grows fast. Her leg heals, and she does not fit in the basket. She is put out with the other chicks, but Chibi is not happy among them and waits at the door for the boy to come home. The boy brings "Chibi" into the house, and puts her in front of the mirror. Chibi the chick starts to sing, "Chip, chip, chip" and our son is happy that he cured the chick.

Our Children Had No Grandparents

Daddy's father fell as a hero
in 1914 in the First World War.
Shortly after, my daddy's mother
from heart failure passed away.
When I was four years old, Mommy's father
had a massive stroke. He also passed away.

Mommy's mother, a sweet bobbe*, was alive,
so I had some love from a grandparent.
But my children had no grandparents.
As they grew I was ashamed to tell them
that their grandparents were massacred
during the storm of the Second World War.

In the spring of 1942, my daddy was drafted
into a forced labor camp.
His unit was taken to the Russian front on foot.
They had no food or warm clothes. Then came winter.

My dear father, at the age of thirty-seven,
was burned alive in a forced labor camp.
The sadistic Hungarians poured gasoline
around the trailer and put a match to it.

My mother, brother and I were deported
to Auschwitz-II/Birkenau in the spring of 1944.
My brother was too weak, so Mommy was holding
him in her arms. They were selected to the left.

I was next to my mommy and brother.
Someone pushed me to the right.
I waved to my loved ones and ran to catch
the group who were directed to the right.
I never saw them alive again.
My mother was a pretty thirty-seven years old
and my brother was five. I was old, fifteen already.

Our only crime was that we were born Jewish.
My children were robbed of grandparents' love.
My husband's mother of natural causes passed away
in 1937. My husband's father was murdered
in Auschwitz-II/Birkenau at the age of seventy-four
in the spring of 1944. By Nazi standards he was old.

Our children had no grandparents to let them do
things that I was allowed only at my granny's home.
My children did not have a granny, to sit on her lap
and listen to stories. The sweet love of at least
one grandparent from my children was taken away.
I was lucky to have a grandmother who loved me.

*bobbe: loving nickname for a grandmother.
In different parts of Europe, bubbah, bubbe, bobby, babby.

Why I Was Not a Child or Teenager

As soon as I was born, I am sure my parents had a hard time. They had an extra person to feed and take care of. I remember one of my aunt's stories: My aunt said, "Your mother complained to me, 'My child looks like a cat. She is ugly, skinny with wrinkled skin. Why doesn't my daughter look like other little girls?'"

But my grandmother was happy. For a week she bathed me in milk. Because of my grandmother's love and devotion towards the new baby, G'd listened to my mother's cry. I grew up fast, strong and chubby, with blue eyes, curly blond hair, red cheeks, and extremely white skin. Strangers turned their heads toward the little girl dressed in pink or blue.

In war-torn Europe I wasn't a child. I was treated as an adult and learned not to complain or ask for anything. Life in Europe, especially for Jews, became worse each year. Soon it was miserable. The hardship continued. Up to the age of ten I was not a child. Then hate towards Jews reached a higher level—the drafting of our fathers, brothers, cousins and soon the deportation of all Jewish people.

Thereafter, I was not a teenager either. Everything dear to me was taken. My parents, brother, home, childhood, my teenage and young adult years. Whom can I ask to give me back the security of a home that was robbed from me? The law and the courts condemn the criminals. Who committed this crime? Whom can I call to court?

Left Our Homeland for the Unknown

With tremendous effort we moved to a big city. Our new home had a large garden. I dug holes in the back yard to plant forty assorted fruit trees and thirty roses on the front yard. With love, I watched how they grew. When they bloomed, it warmed my heart. I felt flowers and trees grow and bloom from my blood.

Unexpectedly, one day we got visas to leave our native country, our city, our home, our garden. The man who got our house demanded some changes in the house. To get visas, to give away our home, by the law, we had to pay the city for changes, for painting the house. The city took possession of our property without any compensation. With worry for the unknown, we gave away the key to our house.

Left our homeland for the unknown, with no valuables, no money. The two children were all our wealth. Many sleepless nights in Italy, we waited six months to get visas to enter into the U.S.A. We arrived on March 17, 1966. It was St. Patrick's Day. Everyone celebrated this holiday, but we did not. Our worry continued. Where do we sleep, how do we feed the kids? No language, no home, where do we go? In a new country, what we will do?

With time, our worry passed. It did not matter that we worked sixteen hours a day. Our struggle gave the children a better life. Bless the day we got to the United States. America is the best country in the world.

The Sun Was Shining

The sun was shining above the meadows, above hills, and above the playground, where Jewish children were playing. Then the sky got dark and the sun did not shine. It hid behind clouds and it got dark. The meadows got dark; the hills got dark. Jewish children did not play on the playground. Where did they disappear? Those beautiful Jewish children with their young mothers were forced into cattle cars.

Without food and water, not even air, they began a long journey to Poland. Those beautiful Jewish children with their mothers were gassed and burned by the Nazis and their collaborators. In Auschwitz-II/Birkenau children were gassed with Cyclon B. Others were murdered with a bullet behind their ear and some were thrown alive in the crematorium oven, or in the adjoining forest, in the ever-burning deep ditches.

The sun hides behind the clouds. It does not shine above the meadows, above the hills. There are no Jewish children in the playground. It will take many generations to forget how Jewish children were wiped out and murdered in the killing fields.

The sun will shine again on the playground, above meadows, above hills. The Jewish nation will be reborn. We won't let darkness happen again. We will be strong and protect our children. The sun will shine on Jewish children forever.

We, the remnants of the European killing fields, lived to see with pride, our small and beautiful country, the State of Israel. The sun will shine on Israel forever—the only Jewish homeland where long ago, our forefathers lived and prospered. Jews live free on our only homeland in the State of Israel. On the Jewish nation the sun shines again.

Arrival at Ben Gurion Airport

In the 1960's my husband and I arrived on an El Al flight in the State of Israel for the first time. Our plane landed in Lod at the Ben Gurion International Airport. My emotions were overwhelming. I wished to kiss the ground and sing. Tears poured from my eyes. We arrived in Israel, our homeland. We Jews, we have a country. No one ever can say to Jews, "You do not have a homeland." Jewish people have a country. Israel is our homeland. Proudly we can say, "We have a country." From the four corners of the earth Jews arrive in Israel to see our homeland.

As we tried to find transportation, it suddenly got dark. In our beautiful country Israel, there is no sunset. The sun goes to sleep early. Daylight is gone in the Jewish homeland in seconds. It was scary that it got dark so fast. The emotion of our arrival into the Holy Land started to evaporate. We had to leave from the airport. But how? My earlier emotional happiness began to fade. Everyone spoke Hebrew, but we did not. How would we communicate with others? In the 1960's few taxi drivers spoke English. A police officer on his radio made one announcement. I worried what he said.

Suddenly a mini-van appeared. The driver spoke English and took us to our destination. Early the next morning the sun rose quickly. The sky was bright blue with some clouds, but in Israel the clouds seldom bring rain. I felt remorse and guilt about my worries. Yesterday's bad feeling evaporated. I was happy to be in Israel, our sunny homeland.

Israel Independence Day

For us Jews all around the world no matter how rich or poor we are, the State of Israel is our pride. Now that we have our beautiful country, The State of Israel, Jews can have the assurance of living in peace without any worry in any part of the world. Around the globe, in any country we choose to live, we can speak any language. Israel is our home and protects us Jews. It will not permit tragedies to be repeated of the almost forgotten past history. European Jews suffered when the Nazis rose to power between the years of 1930-1945.

In 1998 at Latrun, I had the privilege, with my fellow Jews from around the world, of celebrating the Fiftieth Independence of the State of Israel. In my life, it was a most joyous and beautiful day. A thought passed through my mind: Oh G'd how many young Jews gave their lives for this beautiful day? As a child survivor of the Shoah* I understood how important it is for us Jews to have a homeland, a State that can protect us no matter in what country we live. In the recent past Jews were persecuted without mercy; Jews had no country to protect them.

Seven thousand five hundred of us marched through Poland's blood soaked land, where every flower, tree, and blade of grass grew on massacred Jews' blood. None of us will ever forget the celebration of Israel's Independence. We, the few survivors, enjoyed the dance of beautiful young Jewish children.

*Shoah: Holocaust

The Wailing Wall

His Excellency The Holy Pope John II places his secret wish between the cracks.

In my childhood I heard Jews say, "Next year in Jerusalem, we will pray at The Wailing Wall." Jews for hundreds of years wished to pray at The Wall. These large stones are remnants of the Great Temple walls. Jews flourished when it was built. These are very important walls. They show where the old temple was. Many years ago our ancestors prospered in a free state. Tragically the temple was destroyed. At the remains of the Temple's wall Jews and Gentiles alike pray to G'd.

From many parts of the world young and old place their wishes between the cracks of the walls. We place notes of our secret wishes and ask forgiveness for our sins. We pray to G'd for his blessing to give us good health and peace in the land of the State of Israel. G'd bless our country, our homeland, to flourish again as it did long ago.

Around The Wailing Wall is a large courtyard surrounded by tall stone buildings. The tops of the walls are decorated with blue and white flags. The wind blows the flag of Israel. The white and sky blue flag whispers that G'd will help us Jews to come to pray and ask His blessing. Our country forever will flourish. G'd will bless Israel, our homeland.

We Jews come quietly to The Wall, to cry, pray for a strong Israel, to have peace in the Jewish homeland. G'd help us Jews to have a country, a free State, Israel, our homeland.

Whose Shoe Was the Red Sandal?

In the large pile of leather shoes,
behind the unbreakable glass,
a red sandal stands out in the display.
Only one shoe, where is the other one?
Who wore that once good looking sandal?

Where is the other sandal from the pair?
In this huge pile of victims' shoes
the other shoe in nowhere to be found.
The owner is not searching for her shoe.
Maybe she is long gone from this world.

By fate she could have been selected
to the right which meant a temporary survivor.
Why did she never return to look for her shoes?
Where did she disappear? Where did she go?
What was her fate? Did she suffer?

Who was the owner of the red sandal
with the small white trimming? One can see
it's a small size and once looked good.
She had to be young to have a red shoe.
Who knows where she was sent on arrival.

Was the girl's fate the gas chamber
or was she selected to the right,
which meant only temporary survival?
The long hours of roll calls, the food,
the smoke in the air, the daily misery.

Occasional beatings, our shaved heads,
our bodies covered with rags. Often rained.
It felt like a thousand needles struck our bodies.
Many got sick. The Nazis calculated that a
healthy person would survive six months.

On arrival at the first bath, we placed our
belongings under numbered hooks. None of us got
our clothes, shoes or other belongings back.
They were packed and shipped as bonuses into Germany.
For these shoes on display the time ran out.

The Russian army liberated the camp. The Nazis
could not ship the piles of victims' shoes.
They remained as witnesses of the Nazi era.
The red sandal with white trimming stands out
in the display. Where is its owner?

Whose Hair Is on Display?

Behind a glass wall a huge pile of grey hair is on display. It's the silent witness of the treachery done by Nazis. There must be a trainload, or perhaps two trucks of grey hair on display. Whose grey hair is collected behind that large glass wall?

Our Martyrs' hair turned grey, because their heads were shaved after they were murdered with Cyclon B gas in the gas chambers. My mother's hair was wavy, black. She was gassed on the day we arrived in Auschwitz-II/Birkenau. It was June 2, 1944. Is my mother's hair in that pile?

The large piles of hair are the silent witnesses of Nazi crimes. The Martyrs were robbed of their possessions, even after death. In Poland, in Auschwitz-I, Block 18, on the second floor, behind a large glass wall there are piles of grey hair on display.

Old and young hair was used by the Nazi war machinery. Human hair in large sacks was transported into Germany. Hair was used for mattresses and was woven into materials. Then it was given as blankets to the faithful Nazi believers.

My hair was long and blond. It was braided in two ponytails. My head was shaved, so my blond hair did not change its color. Maybe it was woven with other slaves' hair for blankets. Did those who received the blankets know that it was made from slaves' hair?

Hair of the victims, found after the liberation on the camp site.

Luggage Is the Silent Witness

Austria, Belgium, and Holland were under Nazi SS occupation. Every country under Nazi oppression was ruled by the Gestapo's office. The Gestapo ordered Jews to pack their valuables into a small piece of luggage, because they were to be resettled. The people were told to "Bring the tool you need to work in your trade." Further Jews were told, "Make a list of your possessions, so no one can take your valuables." Germans were a trustful nation.

Nazis were masters at misleading people. In each occupied country there were local collaborators who helped the Nazis. Jews hurried to banks to withdraw their money, jewelry, documents, paintings, other valuables, and necessary tools. Carefully they were packed in carry-on luggage. Doctors put in medications; tailors, needles; shoemakers, hammers; lawyers, typewriters. Locksmiths and carpenters packed tools.

On arrival in Auschwitz-II/Birkenau, as Jews disembarked from the box cars they were directed to the gas chambers, murdered and cremated. Jews never saw their carefully packed luggage. The Nazis used the packed valuables for their war expenses. Jews' tools and instruments were carefully sorted, packed and then shipped into Germany. When the war was coming to an end the Nazi SS soldiers had no time to destroy the leftover luggage. So luggage remains the silent witness to the treachery of the Nazis' crimes.

The shameful past can be seen on display. In Poland, Auschwitz-I, in Block 18, on the second floor, there are many victims' luggage, with the owners' name and address. Some wrote an inventory of the contents of their luggage.

Listen to the Winds

Tall trees bend in the winds.
Leaves whisper
and birds fly to the open sky.
Those tall trees remember
what they have seen.

The winds whisper that
fifty-six years ago they witnessed
the local Poles help
the Germans force Jews
from Tykochin
to get on trucks.

Surrounded by armed
and screaming soldiers,
they arrived in the forest.
Jews were lined up on
the sides of three ditches.

Men, women, young adults,
and mothers who covered children's eyes,
so as not to see the deadly guns.
With no mercy, they were shot
until all fell into a ditch.

The butchers had their feast.
Some Jews were mortally wounded,
but the killers did not
want to waste another bullet;
they let Jews suffer until death.

Listen to the winds. Trees bend
and remember what they had seen
when all Jews from the small town
of Tykochin were murdered.
They lay in three common graves.*

Trees get new leaves each year,
grass covers the ground, and birds
fly over the graves. But the Jews of
Tykochin are gone. Even now Tykochin
looks like a ghost town.

A child, an eleven year old boy, fell into a
small hole, and by a twist of fate or miracle
he survived, having witnessed how
Jews from Tykochin were killed.

*I visited the graves in 1998.

Mother with Her Child

In the blue sky,
the sun shines bright.
But for some it is always dark,
even in the bright sunny light.

The sun shines on a stone mother
who would like to save
her child from the certain
death of Cyclon B gas. . .

Or death by fire
in the heated ovens.
Small children
SS soldiers threw in alive.

A mother with a stone heart
would prefer that G'd
send an angel from heaven
to take her child.

With her arms, the mother
holds up the child
so that the angel can
easily catch her child.

Maybe the angel's wings
are broken and it cannot fly,
to take the child from the mother's
arms into Paradise.

Her child remains free prey
in the sadistic killers' hands.
The mother prays, cries, begs G'd:
"For my sins, do not punish my child.

He is innocent, please have mercy
and send your angel to take him.
Please G'd, create a miracle
and save this pure innocent child."

But the miracle did not happen.
Perhaps the angel could not fly.
In rain or sunshine the statue of
mother and child forever stands.

Majdanek, Poland (1999)

Enclosed Courtyard

Newly erected brick and stone walls enclose their inhabitants.
There is no way for anyone to get out between them.

No one can climb over the wall.

The top is covered with pieces of broken glass.
If one tries to climb the alarm will go off
and soldiers with their rifles will kill him.

If one would be a snail, or at least an ant, a worm, or a bug,
no matter how slow, one could climb over the wall,
which is over twelve feet tall.

None can get free
from the newly erected tall brick and stone wall.
Enclosed are our brethren
who are beaten and starved to death.

When a bird flies to the top of the brick and stone wall,
it can see people starving on the courtyard ground.
They lie next to one another.

If only one could turn himself into a bug or into a bird
that can fly over the brick wall.
To be free as a bug or a bird!
But there is no miracle to change a human into a bug
or into a bird to fly over the courtyard's wall.

They can not get free
from the newly enclosed
courtyard's miseries.
There are parents who watch their dying child,
even though a parent would willingly give
his own life to save his starving child.

Parents are helpless.
They can't get food or free their child
from the enclosed courtyard.

Birds in Majdanek

Four birds are on top
of a tall stone pole.
Their wings are knotted together,
with their heads each looking
in different directions.

To the east, to the west,
to the south, to the north,
these birds attempt to fly away
somewhere, anywhere, to escape,
to be as free as other birds.

On the horizon is the city of Lublin.
At night shines its light.
During daylight the birds can see
the beautiful city of Lublin.
There other birds fly free.

The city is only minutes away,
but armed guards beat
and kill birds who look that way.
The birds wish for a day or two
to visit the city to heal their wounds.

To get some strength,
to endure the misery they have:
hunger, beatings, daily killings.
The birds wish to get, at least,
a short break from this hell on earth.

The birds are enclosed in dark
and crowded wooden barracks.
Their lives are miserable.
Often they are beaten.
They have no food, no water.

In memory of prisoners in the Majdanek concentration camp, there is a statue of four birds, perched on a pole, joined together.

City of Lublin, Poland

(continued)

Poor birds, their bloody bodies
are covered with open wounds
and their feathers are torn.
The four birds wish to fly away,
to any four corners on the earth.

Their wings are tangled with each other's.
They cannot free themselves
to fly east, west, south or north.
All four birds must die
within the enclosing barbed wire.

My Vision in Sandomierz

On the large stone-paved plaza, surrounded by nice buildings, I was listening to a Polish man's tales.* But it was not a story; it was true. It happened in August 1943.

City officials summoned all the Jewish leaders of the town for a chat. They forced the Jews into a truck and took them into a nearby forest. Each ended up with a bullet in his head.

Jewish leaders had no chance to warn their families and other Jews in the town, to tell them to organize, to try to fight, or run away. Next day at sunrise, in the early morning, every Jew in the town had to come to the paved square: elderly, women, men, young adults. Mothers carried their crying children.

It happened fifty-six years ago. How frightened they were. I feel, hear, their hearts beat. Not for long could they see the bright sun in the sky. From the windows the bastardly butchers sprayed bullets into the crowd until everyone fell to the ground.

For days blood seeped on the stone-paved square of Sandomierz. A few Jews managed to hide in the tunnel, but bloodthirsty Poles went after them. Locals had no remorse until all Jews were killed.

But, in Sandomierz, one was spared. A young boy was sent by his father to close their door. As he returned, the massacre had reached its peak. Poor child, he ran to the next town to tell what he had witnessed.

*On 4/14/99, I listened to the Polish man's story, closed my eyes and envisioned the tragedy which happened many years ago.

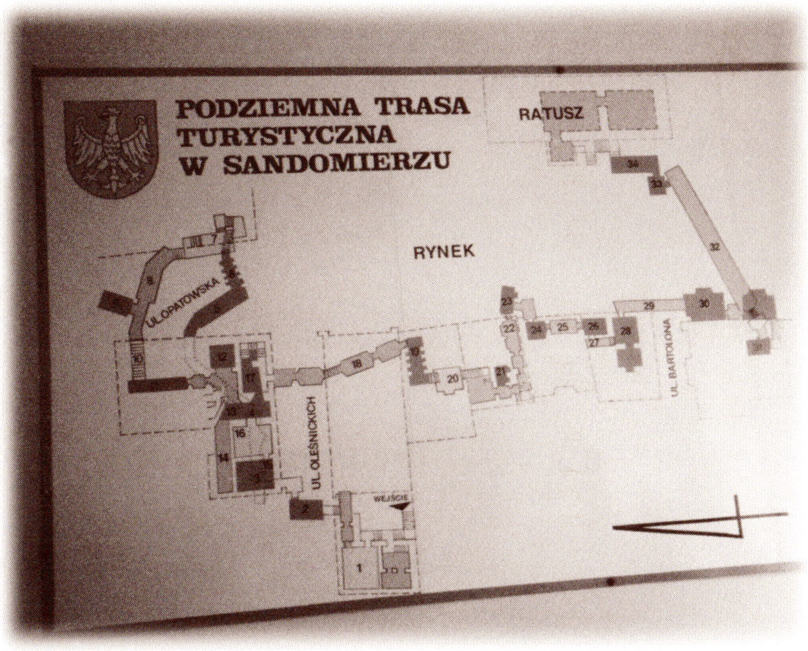

Treblinka

Janus Korczak ran the orphanage in the Warsaw Ghetto and chose to go with the children to Treblinka rather than accept the Underground's offer to rescue him.

1

2

The name "Treblinka" is impressive. One would think of a Polish city or town where people live in harmony, children play and go to school. Each spring green grass, tall trees and colorful flowers show the beauty of Polish land. In the winter a white blanket covers the meadow.

Amidst nature's beauty, there is a narrow partially paved two-way road which gradually changes to one-way and ends on an unimaginable field. On the side of the road, at about a distance of every two meters, are concrete bars. They look like picnic tables on the ground for people to relax on weekends. Big "umbrella" trees spread shade over large cement blocks. Grass and colorful flowers cover the ground. In this picturesque place during the Second World War, a concentration camp was hidden where Nazis, Polish and Ukrainian collaborators brought Jews of Poland's cities and small settlements to be murdered. Jews in Poland were killed like flies.

In Treblinka Janus Korczak, holding orphans' hands, went with them to death. On Treblinka's grassy field and trees, as an aftereffect of heavy rain or melting snow, fragments of human bone grow like mushrooms. One never knows when a bone fragment will appear. In memory of those who perished, seventeen thousand stones are placed on a huge field. Their size varies as large or as small as the town's Jewish population was. Some cities' names are painted on the stones.[1] At the center of Treblinka is a memorial. And as a reminder of the Nazi era, in front of it is a chilling field of human bones covered with ashes and tar.[2]

A Former Paratrooper

On November 22, 1999, I waited in a store to be served. Suddenly a man began to talk, and he proudly said, "In Germany, at the age of eighteen, I volunteered to serve my country." He continued, "I was a paratrooper in the army and fought through to the end." To me, as a Holocaust survivor, his statement was too much. It was more than I could swallow.

Gasping for air, I finally said, "You fought against our beautiful country, the United States. Why did you come here? Germany is your country." And I continued. "You served the murderers, of European nations; why are you in America?" The former paratrooper's eyes were flashing. He got angry, but kept quiet.

I could hardly compose myself and I thought, "How a man who helped to burn towns, who served the murderers of innocent people—how can he live and prosper among us?" As a paratrooper he served among the first group of those soldiers who invaded other nations' lands. Maybe the German Government is rewarding him with a pension. This man killed American soldiers. Why does a former murderer live here? How did he get a visa to enter the United States of America? Who was his accomplice?

Who is he, American or Nazi?

Celebration in Cesarea

The emotional journey in Poland ended. From around the world Jewish children, chaperons and small groups of survivors of the Shoah* arrived in Israel. Israel is every Jew's homeland no matter what part of world we live in. Israel, small but strong, is the pride of every Jew in the four corners of the earth. There were over seven thousand in our group. We arrived to celebrate the Declaration of Israel Independence. The celebration was held in Cesarea.

The festival was organized on the seashore and there was a cool breeze from the sea. There were tables with chairs and a variety of hot and cold foods, plenty of soft drinks and ice cream.

The most memorable event was the celebration of young Jewish children dancing on the theater's stone-paved floor, which was built by the Romans one thousand years ago. Around the theater's floor were stone benches, where the Romans watched shows years ago. Now, on the floor Jewish children were singing and dancing. The change in history provides a great feeling.

At the closing ceremony "Hatikvah"** was played. The music and the voices of over seven thousand people singing. Tears were streaming from my eyes. I wished to hear the song again. I was so happy to see Jewish children celebrating in the former Roman theater of Cesarea. G'd helped the Jews to have a country, a State which protects us around the world. I enjoyed the change in history.

I tried to forget the tiring long trip in Poland: the emotions on the blood soaked grass, the Ash Pond, the concentration camps.

*Shoah: Holocaust

**Hatikvah: Israel's national anthem, "The Hope" when translated into English

Going to College

In my youth, I had no chance for a higher education. When opportunity came in America, I registered at a college. My English wasn't the best, and my pronunciation was a disaster. In my first year, I had to repeat the English class. For us who were born in foreign lands, it takes tremendous effort to speak and write English. In the English language, you swallow some words.You do not read every letter or you pronounce them in a different way.

But I must learn; I am in a college. Often I asked my professors for advice and help. How can I quit school? Their encouragement kept me going. We live in the United States, in this beautiful country. If we don't understand English we are not real Americans.

There were not too many grannies in my classes. It was hard to attend school with a much younger generation. But I made it.

The Golden Age

Why do people always say,
"It's good to reach
the golden age?"
Our body is tired;
it's worn. So our old
age is not golden.

When we are old,
it hurts everywhere.
Sickness takes its toll
on the elderly, and some
are stricken very hard
when they reach
the "golden age."

In their youth, most
elders worked seven days a
week and saved money for a
house for their golden age.

The government takes care of those
who used up all their earnings,
when they get to their golden age.
Some had an easy life, never worked
too much, never saved; they get free
medication and food stamps when
they arrive at their golden age.

We, who worked hard, must pay for
our medication, food and every need we
have, from our savings for the golden age.
Like vultures above their prey, city and
state governments tax our saved
earnings, which were saved for our golden age.

The young do not appreciate the
sacrifice their parents made,
or the hard work, to save for their
children's better golden age.

When Stricken by a Stroke

None of us expect to get a stroke.* It strikes uninvited when it arrives and it knocks you hard, without mercy, off your feet. You become a baby in your bed, cannot see, nor sit in your bed, nor walk, nor feed yourself. A cloud is over your family's head. Tragedy hits, covers your life. No medicine or doctor can help. Your body is stricken with a stroke, and your family suffers the most. Your relatives helplessly try to comfort your stricken body. For them it is difficult to cope and see you in this phase.

If you are one who survives a stroke, you must learn to walk again, to talk, to eat by yourself. Gradually you see and learn to read. You need constant help every day. The recovery is very slow. You are like a newborn child who begins to walk and talk. On trembling feet, you try to walk and nothing is easy—to get up from a chair, to take a shower. Someone must prepare your food and medication. You try to help wash the dishes but forget how to use a sponge. You wash dishes with a spoon or knife; with a rag you try to sweep the floor.

The way you were, it is a miracle you can walk, put on your clothes, shave, eat, and see to read. In time, you hope your speech returns. The daily therapy helps you to express yourself.

* On January 7, 1999 Ernest, my husband, had a stroke. He can't talk or write and hardly walks. With therapy we try to improve his health and with time we hope things may improve.

The Weeping Willow Tree

Willow trees have many branches and have light green pointed leaves. The willow tree has large and small branches. Each bends to the ground, with its leaves we call crying willow. The weeping willow tree is not crying. It grows everywhere and in each continent. Every tiny branch bends to the ground. The tree looks as sad as if it would cry. Its leaves are a nice light green. A willow tree cannot weep or cry.

(continued)

It grows high and every branch with its green leaves bends to the ground. The tree looks like a gigantic mushroom or like a very large green umbrella.

It is bending its many tiny branches to the ground. We think it cries for those people whom we lost in the past century, during the Second World War, in Europe, in the Pacific, and also for the injured ones. We think it cries for those lost in the recent terrorist attack of September 11, 2001. The terror will remain imprinted in the memory of this generation as long as we live. The weeping willow tree cannot cry for us. But we cry for ourselves. With broken hearts we mourn the loss of people, the financial loss, and the destruction in our beautiful city. Why do people have so much hate that they behave with evil? Do they not think of human loss?

The willow tree grows on water beds, in parks, and in every country. Its light green leaves with its very tiny branches bend to the ground. It looks like an umbrella, or a gigantic mushroom. The leaves with many branches create a peaceful shade.

In hot summers the tree casts shade on the benches where people relax and listen to birds singing. Birds fly between the leaves on the tree branches. Each branch with its leaves bends to the ground. In the shade of the weeping willow tree people relax.

How It Was **Then** (1930-1945) and How It Is **Now** (2001)

Then in Europe, Jews lived in fear and mental anguish from the Nazis. There were plenty of collaborators for the physical destruction of every Jew on the continent.

Now Jews in Israel, since the establishment of the State, are under terrorist attack. Suicide bombers blow themselves up to kill Jews. Many terrorists throw stones at Jews. Few countries help Israel to defend itself.

Then no nation on the globe sympathized with the plight of Jews.

Now many nations are united to destroy terrorism on the globe.

Then Jews in Europe, by the millions, were shipped to be killed in death factories.

Now terrorists have come to our land in the United States to murder innocent people.

Then Nazi terrorists destroyed cities, looted the treasure from every country.

Now the terrorists are stopped and their strongholds destroyed.

Then in Europe every nation lost people. Art was taken and buildings were destroyed.

Now we too have lost many people. The financial loss is enormous. We lost the World Trade Center "Twin Towers" and adjoining buildings in New York City.

Then daily, we lived with constant fear of what tomorrow or the next day might bring. People were gassed and burned in ovens.

Now we live in fear of when, where, or what the next terrorist attack might be. Could it be anthrax bacteria infecting innocent people?

Then Jews were not allowed to travel. By law, curfews were issued for Jews.

Now we travel with worry; the terrorists make us think twice if we should travel. At night we are afraid to go out of our homes.

Then after the Second World War, we were free.

Now the terrorists shatter our freedom. With so many terrorists when will we feel free in the United States of America again?

The Twin Towers, Our Jewel

Photo and Painting by the Author

On the horizon are the Twin Towers, the shining jewel of New York City. From around the world visitors come to see the shining jewel of New York City. If anyone gets lost in the city, they look to the horizon for the Twin Towers and find the direction in which to go. Every American is proud of the Twin Towers. From the observation deck one can see far. Houses in the city look as small as match boxes. People, cars on the streets of New York City, and the boats on water look like miniature toys.

Many of us arrived in America from Europe to look for a better life for our children. America gave everyone freedom of religion and the opportunity for ourselves and our children to accomplish our dreams. New York City is the Capital of the World; it is a privilege to live in this beautiful city. While walking on crowded streets one can see on the horizon America's pride: the Twin Towers of New York City.

Then on September eleventh in 2001 a plane with terrorists hit the first Tower. Minutes after another plane flew lower

into the middle of the second Twin Tower. Smoke and fire crumbled America's pride and crumbled the jewels of New York City.

Terrorists destroyed our Twin Towers. America is mourning the loss of innocent people and the World Trade Center, jewel of New York City. Our Twin Towers and the number Seven magnificent pink marble building are gone. The financial loss is enormous. How can evil men murder so many innocent people, creating without warning such terrible destruction in time of peace. Are they killers or sadistic Devils?

Terrorist hate us so much they are ready to die. Why? All America is looking for an answer. Those terrorists did not care how many children became orphans. America is mourning the loss of many innocent lives. Smoke and fire destroyed the jewel of New York City. Without the Twin Towers how can we find our direction? With magic, even a magician cannot bring them back.

New York City Mourns

Mothers are proud to give birth to a baby girl or a baby boy. Fathers are especially proud if the newborn is a boy. New parents make plans for their baby—how soon he/she will walk and talk. The families are happy and never think how many obstacles parents must face raising the new addition in their home. The new parents proudly take care of the baby and watch their child grow. They take the child to play in the park and be with other children of their age. The years pass by. Sometimes with worry, parents watch their child grow into adulthood, get married, and then have a child.

Tragedy hit the Towers of New York City. With broken hearts we witnessed on September 11, 2001 the sadistic attack and destruction of the World Trade Center. The Twin Towers collapsed with smoke. Fire destroyed the Twin Towers. Many families are mourning the loss of their loved ones. Parents lost their children, couples lost their spouses, and many children became orphans. Every worker came at the early hours, in a hurry to be on time at work. Professionals and people of all backgrounds perished in this monstrous terrorist attack. It was destroyed, the jewel of New York City.

Every person is affected in New York City with the loss of a relative, a friend or acquaintance. There is no trace of those who are missing. Memorial services are held in each borough of New York. We mourn the loss of each person.

The Loss of Our Child Arlene*

We survivors are proud to give birth to a baby girl; it is reliving our own dreams which were shattered by the tragedies of the Holocaust in our lifetime. We are the few who survived who lost parents, relatives, friends, homes and struggled to stand on our shaky feet. We got married, built homes, raised children.

We created a new life for ourselves and for our children. When they asked why some of their friends had grandparents and they did not, we could not answer. The baby girl grew, went to kindergarten, then to school. We did not even notice as she blossomed into a beautiful teenager. She got married and had her own children.

Tragedy hit the Towers of New York City. With broken hearts we witnessed on September 11, 2001 the sadistic destruction of the World Trade Center. Our girl, mother of three teenagers, a lawyer, went to work early in the morning at one of the Twin Towers. Our daughter arrived at work on time. And our girl perished somewhere in this disaster with so many others. We, the parents, are heartbroken and have many unanswered questions.

(continued)

Why we parents lost our jewel, our joy, our pride. She was the mother of three young girls who need their mother. G-d give us strength to bear our loss. To lose a child, to carry the burden, is more painful than to lose a parent. Our baby is lost, is missing. She can never be replaced. Oh G-d, pray for her soul.

* Arlene Fried died September 11, 2001. Her parents, Roni and Mike Josep, are from my hometown Şimleul-Silvaniei, Romania. On October 30, 2001, in New York, a symbolic funeral was held.

The Nightmare of September 11, 2001

Terrorism attack in New York City! The destruction in lower Manhattan! Buildings were burning with heavy smoke. People jumped from windows to their death. The unimaginable terror is heartbreaking. We watched on television with sorrow the collapsing Twin Towers of New York City. It was painful to every person in New York and to every citizen of the United States. Also, people around the world felt sorrow.

As a child survivor of the Holocaust, the fire with heavy smoke affects me deeply. The terrorist attack of September 11, 2001 brings back the memories of fire with heavy smoke of the chimneys in Auschwitz-II/Birkenau.

For days and weeks I was glued to the television. I just could not believe what I saw. How could terrorism happen in our free country? In the United States each of us, as new immigrants, got an opportunity to create a better life.

I felt every family's pain that lost a child, a parent, a friend, a home, and even a pet. Some think time will ease the pain. It is not so. As time passes it hurts more. A loved one can never be forgotten.

When I worked, I did not have time to think. Since I am retired, I have more free time and I relive every episode of the tragic years of 1930-1945, with the daily torture and mass murders of innocent people in Europe.

The tragedy of September 11, 2001, brings back bitter memories of my past, the loss of everything that was dear to me. For days I can't sleep. I feel the pain of every child who lost a parent, a relative. I feel the pain and cry with each mourner. I had to see downtown Manhattan for myself. The destroyed buildings in time will be rebuilt, but the loss of human life forever remains an open wound to victims' families, to friends, and every American.

How Can One Say Thanks?

To: Mr. Mell Weiss, Esq., 1998
Ms. Deborah Sturman, Esq.
Ms. Louis Silverman, Executive Mgr.

The word "thanks" is not enough to say, but it comes from deep in my soul and forever with my gratitude.

The wisdom of the three of you and your associates led the case to remind the world how hate and prejudice creates destruction.

For giving your time to our silent almost forgotten Martyrs, from the bottom of my heart to all of you a special thanks.

You took the necessary steps, so a former child slave could tell others her memories of the Jews' tragedy she witnessed.

During the Second World War Jews in Europe had no value. Our brethren were treated less than slaves, less than animals.

Jews killed by millions as flies. How can the simple word "thanks" be enough to show my feelings for your kindness and hard work.

On this humanitarian project, as a team with your associates, you all worked together tirelessly, hand in hand, to remind the world. . .

That people must tolerate one another regardless of religion, color and race. You reminded everyone of the forgotten past when millions were wiped out.

My appreciation and gratitude for all the work you have done. In the name of other survivors, forever, my deepest thanks.

Part Two: Afterthoughts

New Short Stories and Poems

Shame Upon Us Jews

As a child I could never comprehend why I had to keep quiet and say nothing, even when friends called me "dirty Jewish girl." Often I heard, "Dirty Jewish girl, why don't you wash yourself?" It did not help that I washed myself in a bucket two times, and often three times, a day. The sun burned my face and my arms and they got red. I got blisters after the skin peeled. It was ugly: dry skin peeled and looked dirty, at least I thought so. In the winter the cold weather irritated my sensitive white skin which turned rosy red.

I complained to Mommy about my friends and asked for advice as to how to stop them from hurting me. I did not want to be called "dirty Jewish girl." Mother couldn't protect me from my friends, but she advised, "The best thing you can do, is not say anything. Just walk away." This was my generation's childhood.

I grew up a shy and withdrawn person, who was afraid and ashamed to meet so-called friends. They were Gentiles. According to them I was a "dirty Jew." I thought it shameful to be born a Jew. It was like a disease, a curse you carry, a burden through your life to be born a Jew. I was deserted by my Gentile friends. They never called me to play with them.

On the way to school we crossed each others' pathways. They looked the other way. Later in life some even spat on me. To avoid the daily encounter with them I looked out of our open porch to see if the so-called friends had left for school. It was very painful growing up in that atmosphere, daily to be called "dirty Jewish girl."

Like a disease, a shameful curse for years, I was afraid of my own shadow, ashamed to be Jewish.

Ransacked Homes

As vultures watch to grab a live bird, the neighbors of my hometown were waiting to ransack every home. Although my parents worked hard, they did not have an expensive or luxurious home.

In comparison, what we take for granted in the United States of America, European families were struggling for. They did not have a telephone or a refrigerator. Very few had a radio. On our street one family had a battery operated radio. We children were eager to be invited to listen to stories on the radio. In Europe, in the 1930-40's this was common. In our city there was a theater, but people rarely went to see a movie. Tickets were expensive.

In the 1930-40's people had low income in my hometown. Families were struggling to feed, dress, and shelter their children. Couples with four children lived in one room. During the day it was used as a kitchen and dining area. At night it served as a bedroom for the entire family. Siblings shared the beds. They were not lucky to have enough chairs for everyone to sit at one time.

Our fellow citizens anxiously watched to see how soon the government would force us out from our homes. They had no pity when the crying, thirsty, and hungry children were forced from their homes, because then, they could have a free hand ransacking every home.

Plenty of fellow countrymen and women eagerly assisted the police and soldiers to get us out quickly from our homes. Nothing really had value, but collaborators assisted with zeal the ransacking of our homes. Maybe they got a worn dress or used furniture. Did the ransacking make them happy and calm?

Our Empty Home

I had just turned fifteen; I felt so old, so grown up.
But when they ordered us to go out from our home,
I held my mother's hand and asked where would we go?

Mother was holding my brother's and my hands,
but she could not say where we would go.
Mother embraced her trembling children.

The door opened quickly,
and I remember first seeing a soldier's neck.

The order came,
"Fast, get out from your home."
Quick, we readied to leave our home.

Asking the question,
"Misters, may I take a bottle of water and please
let me take a jacket for my five year old son?"
Mommy was cursed, almost hit,
and she was called with never heard names.

The young man was from our street
with whom, in earlier times, we climbed the hills.

In our hands nothing;
in our hearts, love for one another,
as we walked down our street.

Where do we go?

The sun was shining, but did not shine on us.
Mother, Brother and I left our lovely home.
Father had been drafted two years earlier.

A year later only I returned to our empty home,
as a lonely child, with a broken heart.

Raw Potato and Peels with Sand

Over a half century ago the raw potato was my best food. It is nutritious and along with sand filled my empty stomach. It is hard to digest, so I wasn't hungry. But to have a whole potato, that was luck. In the Ghetto's kitchen I peeled potatoes, which saved us from starving. While we were in the Ghetto, raw potatoes were the main food for my mother, brother and me.

A few months later in Auschwitz-II/Birkenau, with other girls, I was sent to bring the large canister of so-called "coffee." But it came with an unexpected reward. We girls had discovered a huge pile of garbage. In there were potato peels, and sometimes, between the peels, I found a raw potato. It was a gift from heaven. It did not matter that the potato peels were dirty, and full of sand. When the Kapo looked the other way, I picked up a handful and stuffed it into my mouth. So I filled my empty stomach with sand and potato peels. Now and then, when luck hit, I found a whole potato.

In Auschwitz-II/Birkenau, a raw potato was a treasure. I hurried to hide it under my arm or in the other hand for others not to see. I carried it back to the block and gave it to my cousin. She sliced it with a metal strip for her sister, herself and me. She covered the bread made from saw dust with potato slices. My cousin made thin slices. At that time in Auschwitz-II/Birkenau, it was very delicious. Once I said, "When I return home, I will ask Mommy to prepare the same food for me."

I wished I could go home to my parents and go to school. At that time I was convinced that my parents and my brother waited for me in our home. Then we would be together and everything would be fine. I would tell my family how much I missed them, how much hardship I had faced, and how I endured miseries which I experienced alone among strangers. I would tell my family how I wished to see them. So much time had elapsed since I had seen them.

But that was not to be so!!

Cattle Car or Box Car

"Cattle cars"are used to transport live animals or merchandise from one part of a country to another. On railroads or often on ships, the cars are loaded to transport large quantities. The "cattle cars" are also called "box cars." During the Second World War, in the years 1939-1945 in Europe, "box cars" were used to transport people. Most people know them as "cattle cars." They have wooden walls with two small openings in both sides in the length. They are tall; even from inside one could not reach the "window." The "windows" were covered with barbed wire.

In 1944 my mommy, brother and I were forced, with more than ninety-five people, in one of those "box cars." It was crowded; there was no room on the floor to sit next to one another. In a corner under the "window," which was high up, the air did not reach us. We three sat between each other's legs. On that late spring day it was hot.

I was fifteen years old and raised to obey the law. We were peaceful people and the law was against us. I took a chance. I noticed a small crack in the wall. Mommy agreed that with my two inch pocket knife I should try to enlarge the crack. I began to carve the hard wooden wall. Slowly the crack got larger. Soon fresh air came through the hole. We were tired, thirsty, and hungry. The clear air gave us some strength.

Lately I have noticed that young adults have never heard the term "cattle car," or "box car." The above description will help young adults to visualize its meaning.

My Question to the Red Cross

Memorial sculpture

Crematorium doors in Majdanek

The Red Cross is an important organization. It protects people on each continent, looks after orphans, helps families to find lost relatives, and assists disaster victims. We support every function of the Red Cross.

Recently in the news we heard and read that the Red Cross organization is alarmed by how the Taliban prisoners are treated by the United States at Guantanamo Bay. Those inmates have every human right. The Taliban killed their own people. They attacked peaceful citizens around the world and in the United States. They behaved like dangerous terrorists and left many families with broken hearts, not thinking how much the destruction cost. At Guantanamo Bay the terrorists are treated well. They have free food and medical care. Taliban inmates don't need to kill for food. Their life now is better than ever before. The Afghanistan terrorist fighters are safe.

My question to the Red Cross organization is, "What happened in the years 1941 to 1944?" In Europe, people by the millions were massacred on a huge scale, some for daily entertainment:

(continued)

- My father was burned alive on the Russian Front by the Hungarian and German allies.
- Detainees were tortured in labor camps.
- People were taken on death marches.
- Children with their mothers, by the million, were murdered in Auschwitz-II/Birkenau.

Jews were peaceful people, not terrorists. Our only crime was that we were born Jewish. In my days as a slave in the camps, I was never visited by a Red Cross representative. What is the difference between the past and present? Why didn't the Red Cross look into how the incarcerated prisoners were treated? We were not considered humans? We were less than flies, less than worms, or rats. How and why were so many people allowed to be massacred?

The Spider's Mouth

Many spiders prick their victims with poisonous venom. Other spiders create a web which looks like lace from which the victims try to escape. But they are doomed and can't escape the sticky lace which the bloodthirsty spiders create.

Spiders first surround their captured prey with tiny fiber-like lace and then suck out their victim's blood. The victims helplessly stand still. They can't escape.

From their bodies is sucked out all the blood. The spiders are small but smart creatures. They know when their victims cannot move. Without interruption they suck their victims' blood.

Did people learn from spiders to suck blood? Peaceful people were victims of those years. They were misled by their own leaders. European Jews were stranded and couldn't move.

The “spiders” struck Jews and other peoples who were exterminated by the millions, not like the real spiders, that suck the blood of their victims one by one. Large groups of deceived innocents were gassed with Cyclon B. Then their bodies were burned in the crematoriums of Auschwitz-II/Birkenau.

In the center of Europe’s map, the railroad lines led to the center at Auschwitz-II/Birkenau, to the famous factory of death like the spider’s web. People by force were herded in cattle cars and were shipped into the spider’s mouth. Then the center swallowed the innocents.

The blood of the unfortunate doomed completely sucked and sacrificed for the “pure.” The victims’ bodies, still alive, were thrown in the ever-burning ovens, in the same way the spider kills its victims: it sucks out the blood.

Nazis with their collaborators were eager, without mercy, to murder millions of innocents. Victims’ ashes fed and fertilized Poland’s soil. Over a half century later, the remnants of the famous death camp web are visible in Auschwitz-II/Birkenau.

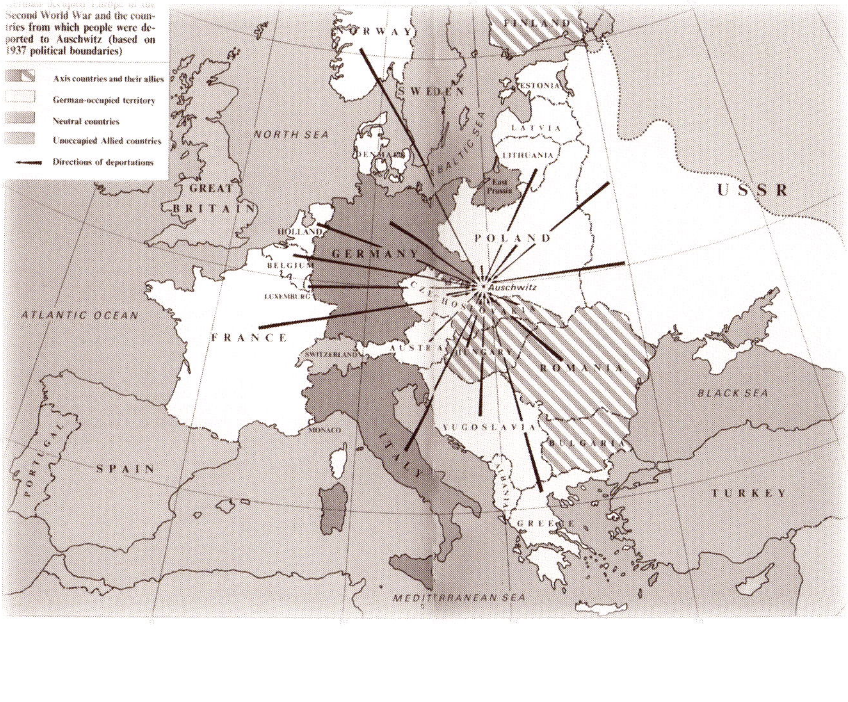

Space Between the Teeth

Josef "Beppo" Mengele

When I see a person with a space between his front teeth, a chill runs down my backbone, and I get goose bumps on my skin. I always remember and picture in front of my eyes, as if would be today, the clean shaven officer with his shiny boots. In one hand his white glove held a club stick while the other glove waved right and left. He looked so neat in his uniform with a half smile on his face, a small space between his teeth showing.

Next to him were soldiers with rifles and barking dogs on leashes. In the background the new arrivals heard symphony music. There was rushing everywhere and everyone was screaming. Naturally it ran through my mind, "Why are so many soldiers greeting the exhausted hungry, thirsty mothers, young adults, and children?" Also, why were the sick, the dead, and the babies thrown on top of each other on a cart pulled by men in worn striped rags? With ashen pale faces, why did they look so scared?

There was no time to think as we lined up. One by one we walked in front of the officer. With a wave of a glove he decided who should die and who should temporarily remain alive. Why did he have a half smile on his face? Was he satisfied that from the boxcar in which we arrived, only I was directed to the right? All the others, including my mommy and brother, remained next to the cattle car. They faced an uncertain fate. We were deceived.

In prior years, like words blowing in the wind, people spoke about horrible things happening in concentration camps. No one believed them. There were stories that on Polish soil SS Nazis and their collaborators tortured innocents, that they killed people in large numbers. Their bodies were thrown in mass graves. That some of their victims were mortally wounded, but the butchers didn't want to waste another bullet. They left the victims in agony.

Some of the refugees who fled to our city told horror stories. People in our city considered the storytellers to be lunatics. In the town, they said, "In the 20th Century barbarism does not happen. People are cultured and civilized."

Murdered Before He Cried

In the 1930's in Europe people struggled, especially those families who had no money to buy food. There was no work, no money. Food was available in limited selection in stores. Because of the Depression people had no work. Even for professionals it was hard to find work, to earn some money for the daily existence.

Due to the difficult situation few young people married. Only a few had the stamina to begin a new life. In this uncertain situation most young couples didn't wish to give life to a child with no future. But some young women got pregnant.

On arrival at a concentration camp a selection was made by SS officers. They waved to the left and right. Left meant murder on arrival; right meant temporary survival. A newcomer did not know the meaning of left or right. It is difficult, rather impossible, to explain how experts deceived the innocent. They often believed a lie, instead of listening to those who predicted the ugly truth.

During my incarceration I heard of pregnant ladies who were directed to the left during SS officers' selections. The SS did not notice women at the early stages of pregnancy and they were waved to go the right side.

(continued)

One day in Block 18 there was some excitement: a woman went into labor. It was time to go out on roll call. We stayed outside to wait for the SS to count us. Miri, our Block Älteste,* arranged that a midwife from another Block come to help the woman in labor. A handsome boy was born, and I heard that the child was strangled before he was allowed to breathe or cry.

At that time I could not comprehend why he had to die. Now I know it was to save the young mother's life that the newborn child had to be killed before he could cry. So many newborn and unborn babies were murdered. A tragedy for future lives that might have been. People who would have benefited humanity in many walks of life.

They had to die before they could cry.

*Älteste: appointee of the Nazis to keep detainees in terror. Some behaved humanly.

Twins or Triplets

Twins are double blessings, especially when one is a boy and the other a girl. Parents are happy to have them. One for father and one for mother. Each will have one to feed, change, and with love, watch grow...to watch their first steps and their first words.

Twins are often born two boys or two girls. They look like two eggs. They can be fraternal or identical. Taking care of a child is not easy. Parents of twins have double worries and big responsibilities, to raise their twins to have successful lives in times to come. To Mom and Dad it is double work. How about when triplets are born? Healthy twins are less of a headache, but when any one gets sick it is trouble. It makes a big difference to hold one child, or twins or maybe triplets. Naturally to feed or change one child is easier than to feed or change triplets.

When twins begin to walk, one parent cannot watch both at the same time. Each twin is an individual person and walks in a different direction. But a mom can run only one way. Who will run in the other direction to catch the other twin who explores everything in his path?

To find what flavor an object has, everything goes in his mouth for evaluation. Oh, oh, something was not tasty enough, but it looked attractive. Let's begin to cry. Mothers or fathers cannot take care of twins or triplets alone. To raise one child is a full time job; to watch twins or triplets two or three times as hard.

For the infamous "angel of death," Dr. Mengele, during the years 1942-1945, it was nothing for his experiments to kill healthy twins or triplets by a lethal injection into their hearts, with the approval of the Nazi regime of those times.

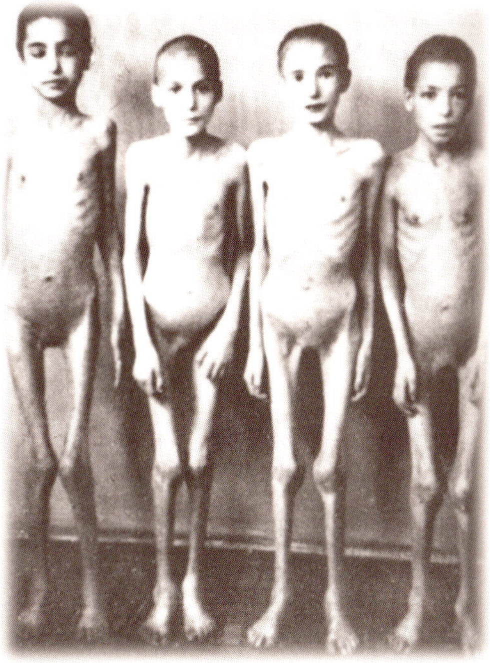

Our Granny's Burial Shroud

Our Granny prayed three times every day
for her children and grandchildren's health,
in memory of her husband who passed away
many years ago. Our grandmother was old.

At least she considered herself old.
We children called her our "Bobbe."
"Bobbe" was old, past seventy-two.
We kids were thinking she is very old.

She bought for herself a piece of white linen.
In the Jewish law, it is customary
for the dead to be buried in white linen.
Granny, for years, saved the white linen.

She folded the material and said to her family,
"This unused linen is my burial shroud."
In the 1930's, in Europe, turmoil began.
Soon soldiers came to take the family.

Granny held the linen. She said to the soldier,
"I want to be buried in this new white linen."
The soldier understood, but a young woman
who was with the soldier said, "No,
I need the white material for myself."

The soldier took away my grandmother's linen
and gave the white linen material to the woman.
The woman was satisfied, but our Granny cried.
She was very upset to be losing the white linen.

The material was about four or five yards.
It didn't have to much value, but for our
grandmother it was a special white linen,
an unused material, which she saved for years.

Granny bought it years ago to face G'd in it,
to face the maker of the universe in the linen.
As a burial shroud, the material had never been in water.
Our grandmother was a religious woman.

Granny was reading books and prayed to G'd.
Though she was only seventy-two,
we thought Granny was old.
She felt the time had arrived to have the linen
as her burial shroud, to enter into heaven.

Why was the white linen taken away from our Granny?

Wrong Place, Wrong Time

It rained often in Auschwitz-II/Birkenau. It was very cold to stay outside in the rain for hours on roll call. The rain felt like a thousand needles stuck in my body.

Many new arrivals with shaved heads caught cold. Some got diarrhea due to lack of protein in the food. On roll call the next day, they were selected and gone forever. Where were they taken? They disappeared without any trace.

Miri, our overseer in Block 18, took pity on us, the newly arrived inmates. Because of the heavy rain on that day, Miri kept us inside in the Block. A group of SS came to count twice daily and select the inmates who looked sick.

A young Czech girl was responsible for us to be ready in time on roll call. On that day Margo Grese, the head of the SS female soldiers, came to count us, to select the sick or the healthy girls for the various medical experiments.

The Czech girl was scared and screamed, "Schnell, Schnell."* With one hand she hit any woman who was close to her reach.

I was nearby. I got a hit on my mouth. For a second, stars sparkled in front of my eyes. I was lucky, I got only one punch. On that day's roll call I was not selected or beaten like other unfortunates. None of us did anything wrong; only some were in the wrong place at the wrong time.

*"Schnell, Schnell": Fast, Fast

A Slice of Bread and a Drop of Water

In Auschwitz-II/Birkenau after the night roll call, a one inch slice of dark bread was distributed. It was such a small piece, heavy and bitter. It had no nutritional value and was made from sawdust. We were so hungry that we did not sense the bitter taste. It was not enough to fill up our empty stomachs. Most inmates, as soon as they received the tiny slice of bread, stuffed it in their mouths and swallowed it on the spot. We hungry inmates eagerly waited at the end of the evening roll call to receive the tiny slice of bitter bread.

The daily hunger created jealously among the inmates. Often the person who was ahead in the line thought that the next one received a slightly thicker slice. It happened between friends and even with relatives, so that miserable days turned even more distressing.

The water was not suitable to drink. It was rusty and yellow, but when one is thirsty one will even drink mud. The water had a metallic taste and many had diarrhea from it.

Food was another source of sickness for the young healthy women. A lukewarm bitter green soup with pieces of sand was given to us. We were starving, but could not eat the green soup. We pushed the bitter soup under the barbed wire for the Czechoslovakian Jews. Poor souls, for years they were incarcerated in Terezin, the so-called family camp.* They arrived at Auschwitz-II/Birkenau with their families. They were only skin and bones, those starved skeletons eagerly waiting to receive the bitter green soup.

Now and then other lukewarm soup was given to us in which pieces of yellow beets were floating. In better days we knew that animals were fed with the same beets.

It ran through our minds, "Could we just be dreaming?" It seemed so long ago that we had real bread to eat and crystal clean water to drink.

* part of the Nazi propaganda program to show the world that Jewish families were not separated or murdered.

Silver Objects in the Sky

As a child incarcerated in Auschwitz-II/Birkenau, I often witnessed small silver objects in the smoky sky. They looked like insects that seemed to fly over our heads. High in the foggy sky those silver objects sparkled and then some objects fell from them. The siren sound disturbed our female SS guard. We were near the kitchen area to pick up large containers of "coffee" in the morning. Our guard ordered the four of us to walk faster. I can see it as clearly as if it happened today. In July 1944 at fifteen years old, I did not comprehend the full meaning of why those silver objects flew high in the foggy sky. History taught us that they were Allied planes that bombed an ammunition factory where slaves of all nationalities worked.

The four crematorium chimneys poured reddish ashes. Smoke that smelled of burnt rubber made a heavy thick fog. Between May 15th and June 15th, 1944, the chimneys spewed high the heavy thick smoke day and night. Also the ever-burning ditches, where our brethren were burned, filled the sky with heavy smoke.

The four chimneys were an easy target on which to release bombs. Why were they not dropped? Who is responsible to answer? It would have stopped the mass killings of the innocent deportees from Hungary, or at least would have slowed down the murder. For this puzzle there is no answer.

As long as I live, I will always think how humans in the 20th century became so evil as to, on such a large scale, murder many innocent children, mothers, and elders. The victims did not commit any crime. They were so peaceful that it was easy to deceive them. Their souls went in the smoke, high in the sky into heaven. Some of those souls could have been saved to watch the sky from the ground and not to enter into heaven. A child, a mother, or an elder could have died peacefully in his home. They could have lived on earth. But those silver objects in the sky didn't drop a bomb to save the innocent or slow down the killings. Why did they not?

Oppression and Hate

Few Jews of my generation survived the destruction of my nation in Europe. Most of those who lived through it are gone. Age and sickness took its toll on their lives. My destiny was to witness the tragedies, to tell the next generation how I survived.

In my view, how was it possible to massacre and deceive so many innocents? The hatred grew gradually for generations and reached such a great scale that the oppression overpowered us. I guess it was my destiny to survive.

Most people work hard, eat at home and don't spend their earnings on drinks. They wish to save something for tomorrow. Those who save try to help their children to reach a better life than they had. With hard work they save and reach their goal. Because of these unwritten habits they dress well and create a better home.

Some people go to bars to have a drink. When they earn something, they feel they deserve it because they worked hard for their money. But half their pay goes down their throats. Most earnings, after being spent on nonessentials, rarely could buy a working couple a house. The rent was high. They got jealous of their fellow men who were able to buy a house and put the children through school.

These and other situations created anger. Officially and unofficially these situations led to the oppression of those who succeeded to create a better life for themselves. Eventually generation after generation, it reached a scary, very high scale, that changed to hate and eventually murder.

In the last century I lived through hate, when oppression reached the highest scale of all time in human history, a time when scared, oppressed people were killed on a huge scale using the most sophisticated science. My destiny was to survive the oppression.

"Black Lake"

At the western part of Germany, there is a forest named "Schwarzwald" (Black Forest). In this forest the River Danube begins. It starts to flow as a small stream and on its course increases into a large river. The Danube River flows through seven countries. It flows through Germany and continues flowing through three state capitals: Austria's Vienna, Slovakia's Bratislava, and Hungary's Budapest.

The Danube flows through the former Yugoslavia and then the border between Bulgaria and Romania. At its end in Romania, it splits into three branches: Killya, Sulina, and Sfîntu George. There the Danube creates Delta Dunări (The Danube Swamp) and ends its long journey at the Black Sea.

In a forest in Romania Pădurea Neagrâ (Black Forest), there is a famous factory that produces special fine quality, colored crystal. It is unique in the world. Poland does not have a Black Forest; it has something much darker. Poland is famous for its many concentration camps.

At the most well known death camp at Auschwitz-II/Birkenau there is a "Black Lake." This lake's water is black. The lake is man-made. There Nazis and their collaborators burned murdered victims during the Second World War.

Between May 15 and June 15, 1944, Jews arrived without stop. The Hungarian government was eager to move every Jew from the countries under their jurisdiction.

The four crematoriums in Auschwitz-II/Birkenau were in use day and night. They still could not handle the flow of new arrivals from Hungary and the territories invaded by Hungarians.

In the nearby forest there was a huge ditch dug. Mothers, children, and elderly were burned in that ditch. Some, still alive, were mortally wounded with a bullet behind their ears. On children the SS didn't waste a bullet. They were thrown in alive and burned in that ditch.

The famous water in this lake is black. It is Poland's unique "Black Lake" at Auschwitz-II/Birkenau. It is sad. The most famous black water in the world is a somber reminder of the attempt to exterminate European Jews.

Miracles Helped Me Survive

I am convinced my survival of the European tragedies, which hit our family and the other Jews in the past century, is due to a chain of miracles. I do not consider myself so special, but without those miracles I would not have survived. I would have perished with all the other children of my age. I survived by miracles.

I was blond, with blue eyes and white skin. For us Jews traveling was forbidden by Hungarian law. Every Sunday I traveled by train to Marghita and at night returned home to Şimleul-Silvaniei. No one ever asked me, "Why are you traveling?"

In the Ghetto of over seven thousand inhabitants, four were ordered to peel potatoes. I was one of them. There in the Ghetto, I had plenty of raw or boiled potatoes to eat. When we left the Ghetto, we were strip searched. I held my pocket knife tightly. I wasn't caught.

On arrival to Auschwitz-II/Birkenau, Dr. Mengele directed me to the right at the last second. Tragically my mother and brother were not.

In Block 20 my group stood in knee high rain water. Assisted by luck, I was transferred to Block 18 to be with my cousins. The next day on roll call I passed out, but an angel held out her wings. Dr. Mengele did not notice. I was taken inside.

From the garbage pile I ate potato peels with sand. It filled my empty stomach and I did not get sick. My tummy was blown up. At the next selection Dr. Mengele pointed it out, but let me go with others whose lives were spared.

In the factory a German Meister risked his freedom and brought me salt to stop the bleeding of my gums. When I coughed and was very ill with high fever, another miracle happened. With a blanket on my back, a German officer didn't beat me for not obeying orders. I was sick and yet not shipped away. Because I was blond?

While on the train returning home a Russian soldier grabbed me. To him I looked German. Because I was blond? I got away. I hid under the bench, behind others' legs. No one in the train betrayed me. I escaped.

My life by a chain of miracles was spared. One last miracle should have come, but it did not. If only one member of my family would have survived. I was alone. Both my parents and my brother perished. There was no one to love and protect me, no one to provide a home for me.

Where Can I Find Some Mazel?

"Mazel" means luck in English.
Why does not everyone have mazel?
When you have your health
and food to eat, it's mazel.

But we humans wish to have
more than just food to eat.
We need some happiness
in life for a healthy mazel.

When two people get married,
the new couple have mazel;
when a healthy child is born
the new parents have mazel.

I wish to buy some mazel,
but nowhere is it for sale.
In a store or in a market,
no one can buy a mazel.

When someone trips while walking
but doesn't fall, it's mazel.
When someone wins the lotto jackpot
and gets rich he has mazel.

But someone who gets sick
and for weeks lies in bed
doesn't have too much mazel.
When he recovers, it's mazel.

Very few are born with mazel,
and others, all their life,
struggle for a little mazel.
Nowhere is mazel for sale.

When children are successful
their parents have mazel.
No matter how much one wants
to pay, one can't buy mazel.

The Four Garlic Cloves

My family and I stayed in Rome, Italy, six months awaiting visas to enter the United States of America.

From older people I always heard that garlic brings luck and lowers blood pressure. Those with high blood pressure do not need medication; they only need to consume garlic.

One day we were notified that our visas to enter the USA had been approved. I went to the market to buy four garlic cloves, so the four of us should have luck in the new country.

I carefully wrapped the garlic cloves and put them in my purse. Our flight stopped for refueling in Madrid, Spain. I checked the cloves and prayed that the garlic should keep away sickness and should bring us good luck in the new land.

On an Alitalia flight we arrived at JFK airport on March 17, 1966. At customs, the officer took away my garlic cloves. He was polite and spoke English, but I did not speak the language. I did not know what he said. Our daughter rescued me. She explained that the USA does not allow anyone to bring in food, and garlic would only cost five cents here.

We were a group of new emigrees of 350 people from Romania. Everyone was happy, but I cried. To me the garlic was very valuable. It was for our luck, for our health. It seemed that no one understood how hurt I felt and scared I was. I felt a chill to the core of my bones. I worried for our future, how my husband and I could provide for our children a home, food, clothing in the new land.

Without the knowledge to speak English, the last string of hope for our well being was taken from us. In losing the garlic, my worry elevated. Others did not understand why I was so scared. If we did not have garlic how were we going to have luck and health?

Our First Work in the U.S.A

On our arrival to the United States of America, the biggest challenge was to find a job, in order to feed and give a home to our two children. In a new country, who would hire a newcomer who doesn't speak, read or write English? In Italy, on the way to the United States of America, an organization provided money for food and shelter, also lectures to learn English. The children learned fast. Worrying how we would feed the children in the new land would not allow us to concentrate on the lectures. We were lucky when my husband's cousin greeted us at New York's JFK International Airport. He gave us $20.00, a loaf of bread, a container of milk, a bag of potatoes, and dinner in his home for three days. And he arranged for us to sleep in a nearby home.

We arrived on a Thursday. On Sunday, with two tokens and a piece of bread, I was sent to work in a factory. On a sewing machine I put together zip-out linings. The dust irritated the constant cough I had since December 1944 when I worked as a slave in Germany. It was like a whooping cough. I choked and could not breathe. My new boss made me tea and I continued working.

In ten days I got my first pay of $30.00. I felt rich. We went to the market and bought food for $15.00. The children attended school and had lunch there. People advised us to ask the government for food stamps. We were too proud to beg for assistance. Our large luggage arrived six months later. The children needed clothes. I bought material for $4.00 and sewed dresses for our daughter by hand. In a few weeks my husband got a dishwasher's job. He washed dishes six days a week without gloves. The rough wire sponge went into his soaked hands. At the take home food store there was plenty to eat, but the owner never offered him a plate of soup.

Our road to create a living in a new land was difficult, but in spite of everything we made it. Still all we would need was health. We worked hard, but were pleased that our fate brought us to the United States of America.

The "Whooping Cough" and Its Aftereffects

As a slave at the age of fifteen I worked for Volkswagen in Fallersleben, Germany. The factory fumes made me ill. First I got a high fever, chills, and back pain; then the coughing. Like a whooping cough with no ending, the shaking of my body continued to last forty-five years.

It was terrible for others to listen to the coughing. Often I covered my mouth with a towel. The doctor prescribed cough syrup in a bottle. It was as large as a two liter soda bottle. I drank from the bottle like an alcoholic.

The continuous cough shook my entire body. The strain gave me a hernia, which got large. I was scared and afraid to submit to surgery. It grew like a balloon, as large as a child's head. Finally I could not walk with the big lump.

The surgeon cut my stomach from hip to hip. With help I could sit or get out of the bed. My bad luck! Suddenly across my stomach, a red line appeared which grew thicker day by day.

(continued)

The surgeon recommended a special corset reinforced with metal to push the ugly red growth inside. It got large like a salami and red as raw meat. The only hope was to return to the hospital to remove it surgically with a second cut hip to hip. From then on I always walked with a support so that the constant cough would not open the two surgical scars. Years later a respiratory infection elevated the cough. After twenty years, the scars split open. A third surgery was performed hip to hip.

Then my old neighbor recommended "Schwedenbitter." It is a product of Sebastian Stroh in Klagenfurt, Austria. A teaspoon daily of this bitter drink stopped the cough. Now it is a headache to procure the bitter drink from Austria. A bottle costs only $4.00. Yearly I need five to six half-liter bottles.

The factory in Austria which produces the drink would not supply it, nor the Volkswagen Plant, in Fallersleben, where I got sick. In the U.S.A. there is a restriction to import "Schwedenbitter." How could I find a solution to get my life support drink?* The "Schwedenbitter" stopped and cured the "whooping cough."

*Friends and acquaintances bring back "Schwedenbitter" when they visit Europe.

Jury Duty

My workplace became very hectic. I wished I could get a break at least for a day or two. Not to travel on vacation, but just to be free of work and have a change of scenery. I would like to see other people outside of my workplace, get some relief from the pressure and tension I had.

One day my wish came true. I was called on Jury Duty. I thought I won't have to work for a while. I felt lucky, as if I hit the lotto drawing jackpot, as if the sun shone on me from under the clouds. I was thrilled. How great! Ready to sing and dance.

I won't have to go to work for two or maybe three weeks. It ran through my mind that my superiors would realize how difficult my work was and how accurate I did it. I never wasted time on conversation while working or drank coffee during working hours. My co-workers often said, "You are disgustingly organized." I took this as a compliment.

In the early morning I waited in a line with many others, to enter the courthouse basement. It was a large hall where we were waiting in a long line to be called for an interview. My lucky day. In a relatively short time twenty of us were escorted to the main building. Then in a hallway we waited again to enter into another room. To me it seemed too long.

Eventually twelve of us were ushered into the hearing room, and we were interviewed individually by a lawyer who asked questions about our opinion on that particular case. Oh, did I feel lucky! I was selected so soon to serve as a juror, but this time the lawyer dropped me. She didn't like my opinion on her questions about the case. I answered very honestly, but often to tell the truth is not acceptable to the lawyers. I was lucky again.

I felt happy, as if the sun would shine on me from under the clouds. What luck! I was dismissed from jury duty and sent home. Afterwards it never crossed my mind that it would be good to have a few days off from work.

At Jury Duty I realized it is true when people say: "The grass often looks greener on the other side, but when you get there the grass is not greener." We must be satisfied with what we have.

A Bus Ride I Can't Forget

I was waiting on a corner for a bus. The orange bus brings me very close to our home in relatively short time. Unexpectedly it was not crowded. There were few people on the bus. At the next stop, a handsome fellow got on the bus. He looked around and sat next to me. I thought, "Why does this young man sit next to me?" There were so many girls on the bus, mainly young beautiful teenagers.

I never fall asleep while on the bus. This time I did, closed my eyes and slept. I can't figure out while riding the bus why on earth I went to sleep. At the Shell station I suddenly woke up and got off the orange bus.

It's only a short walk from the stop to get home. When I got to our house I noticed my pocketbook was opened. The zipper was pulled open wide. The small wallet with my I.D., my parents' and brother's photos disappeared. So the young man took them. While on the bus, I didn't open the zipper. The keys were there. I called the bus company and offered a $40.00 reward for my photos.

Now I realized why the handsome young man took a seat next to an old woman when many other seats were available on the bus. Not to mention all the young girls who wished he would take a seat next to them.

I had only $20.00 with me. The money did not bother me so much, but I felt sick that my parents' and my brother's photos were taken. To me those photos were irreplaceable. For weeks I hoped the mugger would mail them.

This young man was ruthless. He took my money. Why didn't he throw the small wallet in a mail box or leave it on the bus without the money? He did not need my family's precious photos. Since then I seldom carry a pocketbook with me.

The Cobra Is a Venomous Snake

The cobra is a very venomous snake. Unexpectedly, cobras strike people, who die of poison the snakes inject. In some countries where cobra snakes live, natives develop antidotes. People who are familiar with cobra snakes know how to get immunity from their venom. They are protected from its poisonous attack. Others who are victims of cobra attacks die soon from the poison snake's venom.

The cobra's nature is to pounce on its victim and inject it with poisoned venom. The cobra snake with its venom kills its victim. First it lifts up his head while making a noise; then it pushes out its tongue to strike its victim. Few people survive a cobra snake's venomous attack.

Some people look and behave like snakes, ready to attack the unexpected fellow man who gets into his path. A man who behaves like a snake doesn't care if the victim is a child, elder, or an adult. Unexpectedly, he jumps on his fellow man the same as a cobra snake does, often only for the pleasure of destroying a fellow man.

I wish people would not behave like snakes, so a child won't be frightened and mistakenly consider that person a venomous cobra snake. Cobras are ready in seconds to spew venom, the same as those people who behave like snakes.

Around the world innocent people are attacked by terrorists who destroy everything around them. With blind hatred they kill themselves and everyone around them. Who could teach so many terrorists to try to solve their differences peacefully? Not to behave like snakes. Why do terrorists behave and attack like venomous cobra snakes?

A Letter from Singapore

In our country, the United States of America, in the year 2001, there was an Anthrax scare. Many people were infected by the bacteria. One day I received a letter from Singapore. It arrived on Thursday, October 25, 2001. It was a small size envelope, soft to the touch. The postmark stamp was from Singapore. What could be in the envelope and who mailed it? Should I open it or not. I don't know anyone in Singapore. I placed it in a plastic bag and took it to the police precinct.

On Friday morning at 8 A.M. a police officer at the precinct said, "Go home and call 911." "Sir! Please take the envelope from me," I said. The officer replied, "NO." At the next police station, they were friendlier. They completed the information forms. An officer said, "Don't worry we'll check it out and give you a call." With satisfaction I left. My neck began itching and a few blisters appeared. It was 3 P.M. and no police officer called. I drove to the station and a police guard said, "There was nothing in the envelope. It was destroyed."

The rash spread from under my chin to my breast and it itched. It was red like ketchup or blood. At night it burned like fire. I kept ice on it. The next morning our physician prescribed an antibiotic. It did not help. The rash got larger, darker, with millions of pin-sized water blisters on it. I hid the shameful, ugly rash with a triangle scarf. The burning was relieved with constant ice on it. Sunday, a pharmacist suggested an anti-itch solution. Monday, it was darker red with trillions of blisters. A dermatologist gave me a cream. Slowly it got better. As it healed the skin got rough and turned brownish.

No one ever knew what could have been in that small envelope from Singapore. Why did I get the blisters? In the time of the Anthrax scare my case was minor. The red skin and burning blisters were nothing. I would have forgotten about it if the skin would have healed. As a constant reminder of the episode, on the skin of the affected area, tiny dried bumpy marks remained.

Build and Flourish

May 9, 1945 finally was the end of the Second World War. Those who lived through it joyously celebrated. Most European cities were in rubble. In many families loved ones perished. It is human nature that somehow survivors put their lives in perspective, in the best way opportunity affords them. Then they live their lives day by day. War survivors are expected to flourish. Forget war at least for one thousand years so the new generation can flourish. Heal the pain caused by the loss of lives. Rebuild the destroyed cities and bridges. Recover the enormous financial losses.

But evil arises in many people for their personal interest. They agitate other people. Some have goals to be leaders with their selfish egos. Evil drives their egos and they don't care that they destroy another fellow human being. They do not care for others' lives, to leave them in peace to build and flourish.

People wish to live without turmoil. Already two generations have suffered so much. Since the Second Word War in 1945 ended, there is always turmoil someplace in the world. Not long ago it was in Serbia in Europe, Rwanda and Johannesburg in Africa. The terrorists' attack on the United States in New York, Washington, and Pennsylvania.

(continued)

The continuous fight in the Middle East between Israelis and Palestinians. Continued fighting in Asia in Afghanistan and in the Islands of the Philippines.

In the Bible it is written that King Solomon was a wise man. Our globe would need a smart person as he was to solve peacefully differences among the nations. Scientists of this generation can reach the stars. Maybe they will find or be able to create a comparatively smart man like King Solomon. Then on our globe people could build and flourish. Then on our globe their children will flourish.

Could We Forgive or Forget?

The image and date of a group of hungry, dirty people arriving in a cattle car to the unknown is forever imprinted on my memory. Often I wish to forget that week in my life and never picture the starved children. Not to remember mothers who wished to have a cup of water to give their hungry children. The screaming SS soldiers with rifles on their shoulders, the barking dogs on leash, the soft music is forever in my memory. I can't forget the frightened inmates who helped get the elderly, children, young adults, and the sick out of the cattle car.

I see the new arrivals' small belongings thrown into a pile, what they had on their last journey. How can I forget the tall, smoky chimneys? At night when new transports arrived,

I heard children cry in the dark. It felt like a knife stabbing in my heart. How I can forget the memory of those nights?

How can I forget the return to my home city to find out that I was an orphan with no one to love me, no one to take me under their wings. I wish to forget the scary days and nights, when free as a bird, I had only an empty home. There was no one to take care of an orphan child. The orphan who struggled over a year to see the day when she would live without worry and get under her parents' protecting wings.

How I can forget my handsome parents? Could I ever forget my only brother?

Throughout life we must forgive and forget many things, but we can't forgive everything. Can Americans forgive or forget the loss of many lives in the terrorist attacks of September 11, 2001? The many orphans who lost their parents or parents who lost their child, will they ever forgive or forget? The loss of the "Twin Towers" in New York City, could Americans ever forgive or forget? The tragic loss of my parents, brother, relatives and my home, how can I ever forgive and forget?

A Hole in the Ground

Once upon a time there were
Tower One, Tower Two, and other
smaller buildings close to the Twin Towers.
This is a real story, not a tale.
In New York we had two tall Towers.
They were unique in the World.
Proudly they stood in downtown Manhattan
illuminating the entire City of New York.

We who live in New York City always took
for granted that the shining Twin Towers
would stay forever in New York City.
Around the world jealously arose.
And they sent terrorists to destroy
America's Twin Towers in New York City.
In this tragedy families lost their loved ones.
We cry with them forever.

Destruction of the surrounding buildings
created enormous financial loss.
The tragedy of September 11, 2001
is imprinted on every American's heart.
We remember and pray with relatives.
We have a deep hole in our hearts forever.
Where once the Twin Towers stood there is a hole.
It is seven stories deep in the ground.

The hole in the ground is like a crater.
It is as deep as after a volcanic eruption.
It is the grave of innocent people who lost their lives,
close to the Financial Center and Winter Garden.
The people who perished during the destruction
of New York City's Twin Towers
will remain forever in every American's heart.

Years from now, the buildings of the Twin Towers
will be seen only in photos and displays.
An earthquake covered the City of Pompeii with ashes.
In New York City the ashes and the debris were
seven floors deep and as large as a football field.
Future generations will say that, "Once upon a time
in New York City, there were Tower One and Tower Two."

Will New York ever have again its illuminating Towers?

Tears Which Never Dry

From the tragedies of the past century we lived through, our tears did not dry. We are the few who miraculously survived destruction of the "chosen nation." Most survivors of the large scale massacres in Europe are long gone. Age, sickness, and the past misery took their toll and most are gone.

G'd promised our forefather Abraham that He would watch our nation prosper. We obey the Ten Commandments which were given long ago to Moses in the Sinai desert. David and Solomon were peaceful rulers of Judea. We are descendants of Abraham, Moses, David, and Solomon. They ruled Judea (Israel) with wisdom, and under their rule Judea prospered. I wish that Abraham, Moses, David, and Solomon would pray in heaven for a lasting peace. People in our ancestors' homeland should prosper. The State of Israel has never had peace.

Already too many innocent lives have been extinguished, and our nation is bleeding. In the past the world closed its eyes and ears to innocents' cries for help. Though the world is openly against terror, many are also against the State of Israel's existence. Our homeland is our savior no matter which part of the world we live.

Life in Israel is not milk and honey. On the hills there is only stone and sand. With tremendous effort cities were built, but

Israeli people live in constant fear. On Israel's roads daily tragedies occur. Terrorists attack busses, the explosions kill innocent people, and the attacker does not value his own life and dies with them.

From the loss and sufferings of the past our tears did not dry on our faces. Yet with daily loss of our pride and joy, of Israel's youth, our tears cannot dry.

I Climbed a Chestnut Tree

In the city where I was born and lived in my early childhood, every autumn the hills were full of ripe fruits and grapes. We children liked to climb the hills. There were plenty of chestnut trees from which to pick ripe chestnuts to take home. The chestnut trees grew on the hills. Also in the early autumn the ripe blackberries were free to pick at no cost.

The other children were a few years older and much stronger than I, especially the boys. It took nothing for them to climb on a tree branch. I became jealous of those who were in the trees, picking large chestnuts. I began to climb on a smaller tree, but I had no prior experience. I thought if others could climb there was no reason why I could not. As I climbed on a higher tiny branch, the small branch suddenly broke.

I fell to the ground, lost my balance, and rolled down on the hill. I got a lot of bruises and scratches, but luckily no broken bones. Two boys put their hands together and formed a support to carry me down the hill. I was lying on the ground until my parents arrived to take me home. I had a lot of bruises on my body and my left wrist was sprained.

An old lady came twice daily and put my wrist in a bucket of lukewarm water and massaged it. I had lots of pain and was swollen. The bruises on my body hurt. The sprained wrist was painful. It was more painful because, for a while, I could not climb the hills.

Watermelon

It's good to eat a slice of juicy red or yellow melon, especially in the summer when it is humid and hot. The fruit cools our body and takes away our thirst. During the summer season it is not very expensive. Grocery and fruit stores order them from the farmers. By truckloads they arrive in the supermarkets. There are plenty to choose from.

One can buy a whole, half or a quarter, seedless, or seeded, red or yellow. The seeded yellow or red watermelon looks as if it has been decorated with its black or dark brown seeds. Usually in the supermarket I buy a whole watermelon. It is a flashback, a reminder of my childhood.

In the summer of 1942, our neighbor said to my mother, "I bought watermelon in the market." My three year old brother curiously asked, "What is watermelon?" Next day, our mother bought a small slice of watermelon for us.

Luxury items like watermelon or fruits were not on our menu. We were happy to have bread, milk, and baked potatoes for supper.

I will never forget those hard years. In the market there were plenty of melons, fruits, and assorted foods to choose from, but few had money to pay for them.

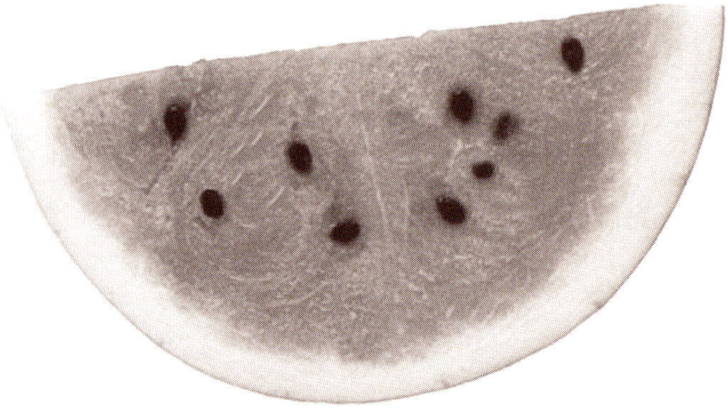

Orange

When orange trees blossom the air is full of their fragrances. Flowers fall and change into small green balls. Balls grow and they turn yellow. Between the green leaves oranges look like decorations on trees. They grow in various sizes and flavors. The sweetest are the mandarin and the small clementine. We all take for granted that there are plenty to choose from in stores. We can buy any type or size of this sweet and juicy fruit. Few of us would think that in the 1930's and 1940's it was different.

For my twelfth birthday my mother insisted that I invite some of my classmates, but not too many girls came. Birthdays were not celebrated. There was no money for presents. I remember Klari, a brunette. She was smart and played the violin. And Jitu, a blonde. They gave me a juicy yellow orange for my birthday. I was thrilled to get this present. One of us peeled the orange, and we all ate a small slice. The orange was delicious. We wished we could have another piece.

My mother served us cakes, biscuits, compote, tea and nuts. We had a good time. My twelfth birthday was gone. The girls left and I never celebrated another birthday. This is not fiction. It reflects my childhood memory.

Valentine's Day

Deep love comes
from the heart.

As Dad and Mom's
child I was close
to their hearts.
My little brother
forever remains
in my heart.

I was born on
Valentine's day
to be my family's
sweetheart.

My left hand is
on the same side
as my heart.

Cruelty of life
damaged my heart.

I pledge with
my right hand
over my heart.

A broken object
can be fixed...

But my damaged heart
can never be mended,
even on Valentine's Day.

The Mouse and Mitzi the Cat

On a rainy Sunday night we went to see a movie. Our children, fourteen and eight years old, chose to stay home to finish their homework. Two and a half hours later we walked home. We heard a screaming in the street that went through our bones. Worried, we walked up the steps.

The kids were on the table trembling, crying, scared. "My G'd, what happened?" Sobbing, they could only say, "There in the corner! It's a grey mouse!"

Where is Mitzi the cat? Perhaps she is having a date with the neighbor's cat. How should we catch the mouse if Mitzi is not around? We called to Mitzi, "Please come. Where are you?" Soon Mitzi our cat returned and in a moment Mitzi caught the grey mouse.

We had seen a good movie, but it was not worth the worry and the scare we all went through. A few months later our cat Mitzi gave birth to four small kittens. For a few days the kittens could not see, but they grew fast. So Mitzi our cat again stayed out and looked for new adventures.

The Author's children, ages 2 and 8

Spoon River

My hometown is named Spoon River.
The town's name is same as the river,
which flows with crystal clear
water in the middle of my hometown.
My town is named after this small river.

The river in summer days is a small stream.
One can walk across the river
from one side to the other with shoes on.
Each spring snow melts, and on the river
people float in small boats and kayaks.

On weekends we children try to catch fish.
When luck smiles on us we catch them.
In the early summer the water begins to subside.
Then we barricade the water with sand.
A stranded fish is easy to catch.
We pick the live fish with our hands.

The City Hall is built close to the river.
Our school is best known for agriculture.
It is built on the right side of the river.
In the winter the river freezes at Spoon River,
and we ice-skate on the frozen water in my hometown.
In the summer and winter people from close-by cities
travel to my hometown for some recreation.

They come to relax, have a quiet vacation,
enjoy nature's beauty, and to rejuvenate
their tired bodies. Each year people return.
My hometown is a picturesque place.
It is built on two sides of the Spoon River.

When I grow old, I will retire to my hometown
and build a house with a large garden.
In the summers I will watch the blooming flowers
and enjoy the air filled with their fragrances.

I will plant fruit trees, watch them grow tall,
blossom in the spring and fruit in the summer.
My trees will last long after I am gone.
The grandchildren will remember their grandfather
because he will have created, for the coming generation,
a lasting place to stay for vacation in my hometown.

There will be a large house in the middle of a huge garden
in which flowers will be blooming. In the shade
of trees will be benches to relax at Spoon River.

*This was my poem in response to reading Edgar Lee Master's "Spoon River Anthology." This is my imagined Spoon River, my ideal of a hometown that might have been.

Blue Sky and Rain

When the sun
shines bright
the sky is blue
and warms my heart.

In the bright
and clear sky
I see birds fly high
to reach the stars.

After a rain
the sun shines.
After raindrops fall
grass grows green.

Flowers bloom
and cover meadows
with a colorful
rainbow blanket.

The air is filled
with fragrances
and the aromas
attract bees.

Bees suck the flowers'
sweet juices
and turn them into
sweet honey.

After a rain
when the sun shines,
often a colorful
rainbow appears
on the horizon.

The clear blue sky,
the flowers,
the flying birds
brighten my day.

Winter

Raindrops are freezing
and snow is falling.
A white blanket
covers the ground.
It is so peaceful
and nice to look at,
out of the window
from the warm home.

Outside it is hazardous
to walk. It is cold
and streets are covered
with frozen snow.
To melt the snow,
day and night,
special trucks sprinkle
every street with rock salt.
Owners shovel the snow
from their sidewalks.
On streets walking
is very treacherous.

When snow falls
children are happy.
They ride on sleds
and make snowmen.
Snowball fights are popular.
Children have fun
and they never get tired
of throwing a snowball
at each other's heads
or someone's window.
After snow falls,
winter fun never ends.

Four Seasons

"Spring is here."
The sun shines,
and warms Mother Earth.
Meadows change color;
new grass makes them green.
In the sky wild geese fly,
assure us that spring
has arrived.
Birds are busy repairing
or building new nests
for their chicks.

In a few weeks,
the weather gets warmer,
nights are shorter,
and days get longer,
telling us, "Summer is here."
In rainbow colors,
flowers are blooming.
Birds are busy feeding
and teaching their
new chicks to fly.

"Autumn brings breezes"
and days are getting shorter.
Hills are filled with fruits
and birds prepare to fly away
to warmer places.
Soon the weather gets cooler
and rain changes to snow.

Meadows and forests
are covered
with a white blanket.
"Winter has arrived."
It puts nature to sleep,
until the next spring.

Nature never gets old;
the cycle is repeated,
year by year.

Every Rose Is Pretty

The Author's children, 1986.

The red rose is one of the nicest flowers. People send at least a dozen roses to their sweethearts for a birthday and for any other special occasion. It is customary to give a card with a bouquet of roses on which love words are printed. It would be more compelling if the giver would write his own words.

Roses ordered from flower shops, blooming or not, are without any fragrance. The following day the new bunches of roses have faded and have never fully blossomed. In contrast, if you have a rose bush in your garden you can cut roses on the day you see or meet your sweetheart. They will keep their perfume for days to come.

Roses have pointy thorns that can scratch skin so deeply that it can bleed. But roses are very pretty flowers, and mothers often like to name their offspring after them: Rose, Rosa, Rosalie, Rosalinda or Rosita. The child is not always as pretty as a rose is. To give a child the name of one of the prettiest flowers is heart-warming. Every girl is happy to be named after a flower which is used by sweethearts and on special occasions.

Roses bloom in many colors. The song "The Yellow Rose of Texas" is one of the most popular songs. Young and old alike joyously listen and dance to its popular melody. A bunch of roses from one's garden, in any color, will fill the room with fragrance. The shape or color of a rose does not matter. They are all very pretty.

My Hopes and My Dreams

My Hopes are:
Health to my family and to us as old parents.
Success for my children and to see them happy.

My Dreams are:
Peace on Earth, especially in the United States
and in the State of Israel.
People never should be hungry.
No one should be homeless.
All terrorists should resign.
There should be no more destruction of buildings,
no more car bombs.

I worry when I watch the news; often I would rather not listen. It hurts to hear that daily, somewhere in the world, many parents, spouses, and children lose their loved ones to terror. We who lived through the Second World War feel the pain of everyone who has lost a family member. For families it is painful when old age or sickness takes one's life away. Family members mourn for the loss of the departed and forever they will keep the memory in their heart. Tragedy hits every family who loses a loved one by accident or terror. A deep hole remains in the family's heart which never entirely heals. The close relatives smile with tears in their eyes and with pain in their hearts. Family members seldom can truly laugh.

My Other Hopes are:
To win the lotto to build an old age home for those
who can't afford an aide to help them.
And a home for orphaned children.

My Other Dreams are:
To live in good health,
never to need
others' assistance for the existence
of my everyday life.

Epilogue

I am from Judetul Sālaj and the city of Şimleul-Silvaniei. I was born on February 14, 1929, when the Depression in Europe was getting worse. Poor and middle class families had to choose whether to buy clothes, a pair of shoes, or food for their children.

During the Hungarian invasion, I kept a diary about how our lives changed and how best friends turned away from us only because we were born Jewish. After the war, I returned home with a hope that our lives would become normal. I was 16 years old and everything disappeared: my parents, my brother and my relatives. Our home was empty. When I received the information that I had lost everyone and everything, I could not think or talk for a long time. I asked myself how our G'd allowed so many lives to be extinguished. I wanted to believe that my parents in heaven prayed for me and watched over my fate, but many times I had doubts.

After WW II, I wished to leave a written memory of my parents, so they should not be forgotten. Since we lived under Communist rule, I thought this memorial would cause suspicion. In my poems and stories, I briefly touched on many major events of my life. By writing these poems and narratives, my goal was to leave something about our past lives to the present and future generations.

I was married at seventeen to Ernest, who is a survivor of various forced labor camps and the Death March. We lived under Communist rule in Romania from 1946-1966. We dreamed of leaving Romania, but for many years it remained only a dream. Finally, we received our visas and left.

In the United States, each New Year passes quickly. With my husband of 57 years, our lives were not easy. In spite of everything, we raised and educated two children. We need only our health. In spite of all our hardships, we have survived.

Elly Gross, née Berkovits
July 2003

Liberation 1945

Photo: EBENSEE, MAY 7, 1945
(National Archives, Against U.S. Army Flags)

On May 8, 1945, jubilant crowds around the world celebrated V-E (Victory in Europe) Day, marking the end of the twelve years of Nazi tyranny, destructive warfare and unimaginable evil. But inside the liberated concentration camps, sufferings did not end, as thousands continued to die from disease and starvation. Many who survived faced the future with fear and uncertainty.

Although reports of Nazi camps and atrocities had appeared in the Allied press during the war, even battle-hardened soldiers were shocked and sickened as they entered such camps as Bergen-Belsen, Dachau, and Buchenwald during April and May 1945. They discovered thousands of sick, famished prisoners sharing squalid quarters with unburied corpses. . . Survivors and U. S. Army veterans . . . recall the first moments of liberation and the difficult days and months that followed.

—From "LIBERATION," a handout for the Special Exhibition Gallery at the United States Holocaust Memorial Museum, Washington D.C.

At age fifteen in 1944, I was deported to Auschwitz-II/Birkenau in Poland, shipped to Fallersleben in Germany, liberated in Saltzwedel on April 14, 1945, in a few weeks transferred to Hillersleben, and then returned home to nowhere.

My husband in 1942, at age twenty-one, was drafted into forced labor and for over three years was in a forced labor camp in Poland and the Ukraine, then on the Death March to Dachau, liberated at Gurckinhen on May 6, 1945, and then home to nowhere. In 1946 we met and then married.

The Liberation photo and article re-printed above reflects our appreciation to the liberators, the American and Allied Armies. We, who survived the unimaginable horror of the 20th century, began to search for what was left of our families. It was a sad and gruesome task down a road to nowhere.

Ernest Gross

Ernest (Erno) Gross
2003

Elly Gross, née Berkovits

Elly Gross, née Berkovits

Maps

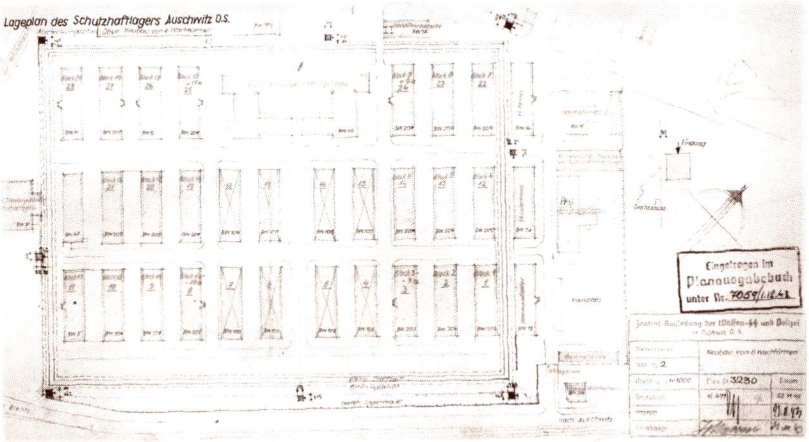

Auschwitz-I: The Archives, Museum Office and Displays

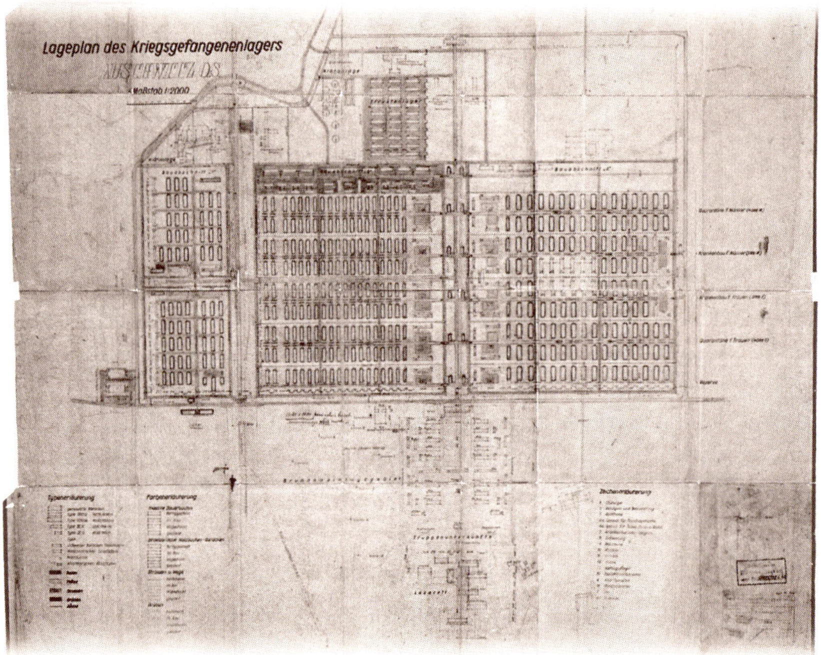

Auschwitz-II/Birkenau: The Killing Fields

Original maps on this page of Pantstwowe Muzeum Oswiecimiu including Auschwitz-I and Auschwitz-II/Birkenau are provided by the generosity of the Director of the Museum Archives, Dr. Piotr Setkiewicz.

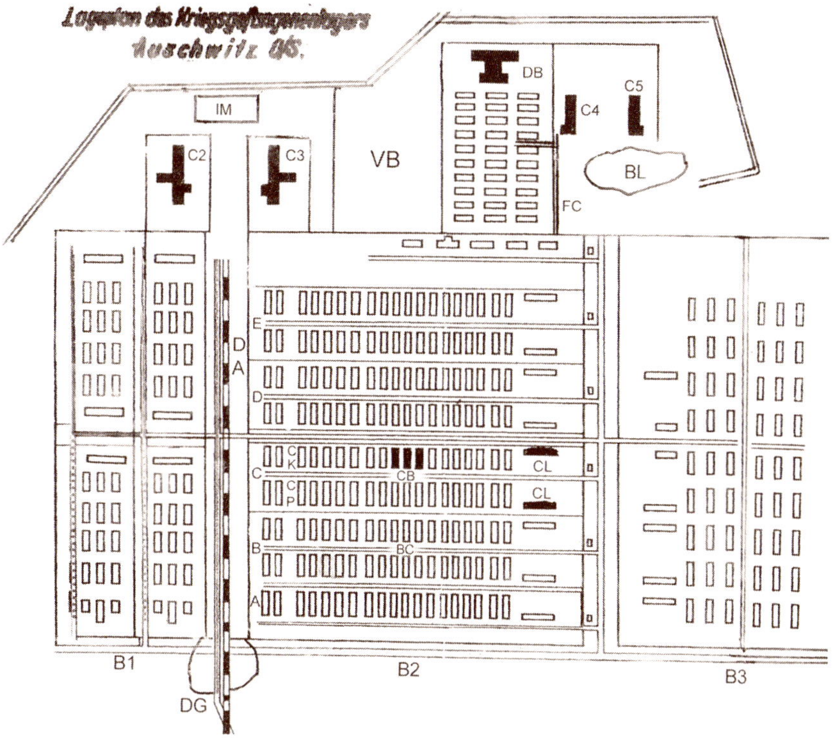

Auschwitz-II/Birkenau Concentration Camp

Notations by the Author indicate the places at the camp where she lived as a slave in 1944 and areas she visited in 1998 and after. Shown are the barracks and the camp areas B1, B2, and B3.

B2. DG.	Death gate, entrance to hell
B2. DA.	Area for arrival and selection
B2. DB.	Disinfection building
B2. C2, C3, C4, C5.	Four crematoriums
B2. VB	"Canada" Area where victims' belongings were sorted
B2. BL.	Black Lake (ditch)
B2. FC.	Fence covered with blankets
B2. IM.	International Memorial
B2.	LAGER C
B2. CP.	Plaza Lager C
B2. CK.	Kitchen/garbage pile
B2. CL	Latrine/washroom
B2. CB.	Block 16, 18, 20 where the Author lived as a slave/worker
B2.	LAGER B
B2. BC.	Czech Jews from Terzin (Teresienstadt)

Yad Vashem—Commemorating the Names Pages of Testimony

This picture is taken from the "Auschwitz Album." The two people indicated in the photograph were identified by Elly Berkovits Gross as her mother and brother who were murdered in Auschwitz in 1944.

On May 27, 1944, Irina Berkovits, age 37, her daughter Elly, age 15, and son Adalbert, age 5, were deported from Hungary. (Irina's husband, Eugen, had been taken for forced labor in 1942. He never returned.) After traveling by train for 7 days without food or water, Irina, Adalbert and Elly finally arrived in Auschwitz. Elly was separated from her family during the selection process. Elly's mother and brother were sent to the gas chambers; Elly was selected for forced labor. She never saw her mother and brother again.

In 1990, Elly Berkovits Gross filled out these Pages of Testimony and submitted them to Yad Vashem.

The "Auschwitz Album" is comprised of photos taken by a German photographer at the Auschwitz II camp (Birkenau). The album is divided into sections with German titles. This picture is from the section titled "Arrival of Transport."

The pictures were apparently taken as an official document recording the arrival of Hungarian Jews in the camp. Shortly after liberation, the album was found by survivor Lili Meir, whose family was part of the transport that was photographed. She donated the album to Yad Vashem on August 27, 1980.

http://www.yadvashem.org.il/remembrance/names/album.html

(copy transcribed from web site pictured below)

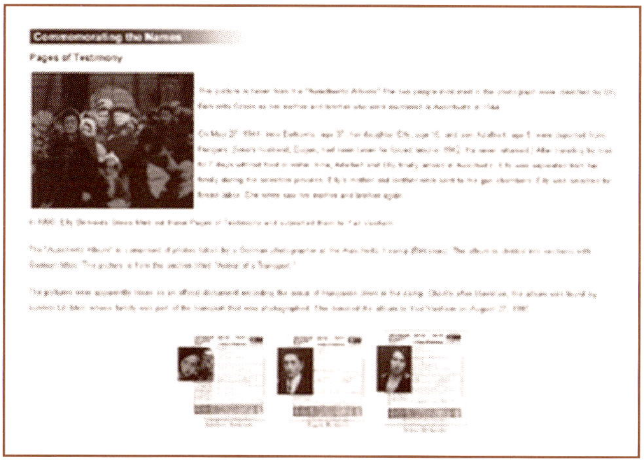
Commemorating the Names
Pages of Testimony

Eugen Berkovits

Irina Berkovits

Adalbert Berkovits

Documents

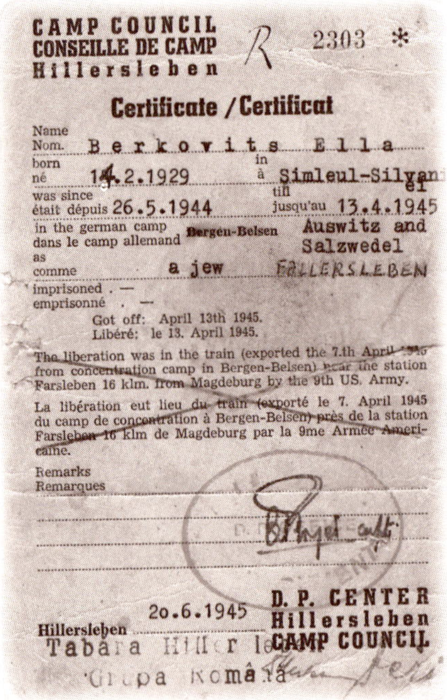

CAMP COUNCIL
CONSEILLE DE CAMP
Hillersleben

R 2303 *

Certificate / Certificat

Name / Nom. Berkovits Ella
born / né 14.2.1929 in / à Simleul-Silyanei
was since / était dépuis 26.5.1944 till / jusqu'au 13.4.1945
in the german camp / dans le camp allemand Bergen-Belsen Auswitz and Salzwedel
as / comme a jew FALLERSLEBEN
imprisoned . — / emprisonné . —

Got off: April 13th 1945.
Libéré: le 13. April 1945.

~~The liberation was in the train (exported the 7.th April 1945 from concentration camp in Bergen-Belsen) near the station Farsleben 16 klm. from Magdeburg by the 9th US. Army.~~

~~La libération eut lieu du train (exporté le 7. April 1945 du camp de concentration à Bergen-Belsen) près de la station Farsleben 16 klm de Magdeburg par la 9me Armée Americaine.~~

Remarks / Remarques

Hillersleben 20.6.1945

D. P. CENTER
Hillersleben
CAMP COUNCIL

Tabara Hiller le...
Grupa Româna

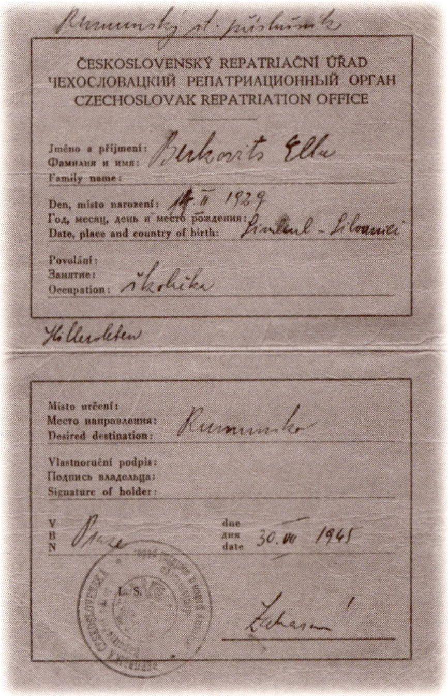

Rumunsky st. příslušník

ČESKOSLOVENSKÝ REPATRIAČNÍ ÚŘAD
ЧЕХОСЛОВАЦКИЙ РЕПАТРИАЦИОННЫЙ ОРГАН
CZECHOSLOVAK REPATRIATION OFFICE

Jméno a příjmení: / Фамилия и имя: / Family name: Berkovits Ella
Den, místo narození: / Год, месяц, день и место рождения: / Date, place and country of birth: 14 II 1929 Simleul-Silvaniei
Povolání: / Занятие: / Occupation: školačka

Hillersleben

Místo určení: / Место направления: / Desired destination: Rumunsko
Vlastnoruční podpis: / Подпись владельца: / Signature of holder:
V / B / N Praze dne / дня / date 30. VII 1945

L. S.

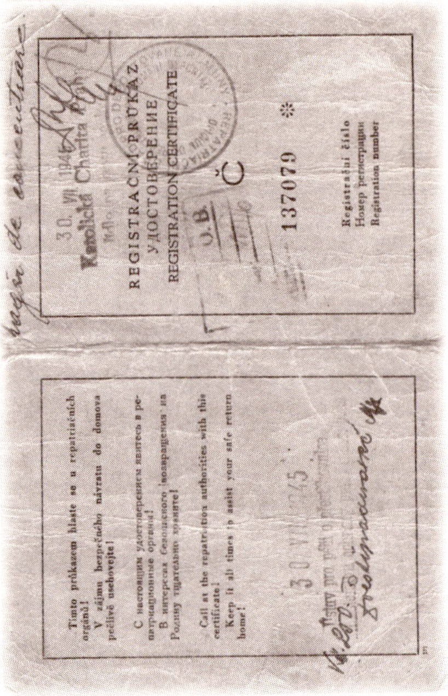

REGISTRACNÍ PRŮKAZ
УДОСТОВЕРЕНИЕ
REGISTRATION CERTIFICATE

137079 *

Registrační číslo
Номер регистрации
Registration number

Tímto průkazem hlaste se u repatriačních orgánů!
V zájmu bezpečného návratu do domova pečlivě uschovejte!

С настоящим удостоверением являтесь в репатриационные органы!
В интересах безопасного возвращения на Родину тщательно храните!

Call at the repatriation authorities with this certificate!
Keep it at all times to assist your safe return home!

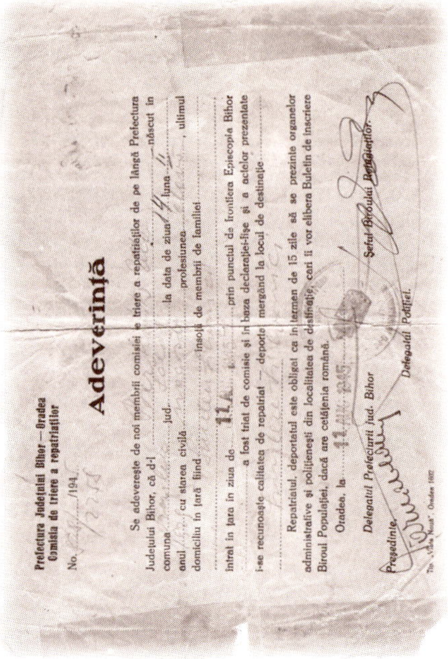

Prefectura Județului Bihor—Oradea
Comisia de triere a repatriaților

No. ..../194..

Adeverință

Se adeverește de noi membrii comisiei de triere a repatriaților de pe lângă Prefectura Județului Bihor, că d-l .... născut în comuna .... jud. .... la data de ziua 14 luna ... anul ... cu starea civilă .... profesiunea .... ultimul domiciliu în țară fiind .... însoțit de membrii de familiei ....

intrat în țara în ziua de 11 .... prin punctul de frontiera Episcopia Bihor a fost triat de comisie și în baza declarației-fișe și a actelor prezentate i-se recunoaște calitatea de repatriat — deportat mergând la locul de destinație ....

Repatriatul, deportatul este obligat ca în termen de 15 zile să se prezinte organelor administrative și polițienești din localitatea de destinație, cari îi vor elibera Buletin de înscriere Biroul Populației, dacă are cetățenia română.

Oradea, la 11 ... 1945.

Președinte — Delegatul Prefecturii jud. Bihor — Delegatul Poliției — Șeful Biroului Repatrierilor

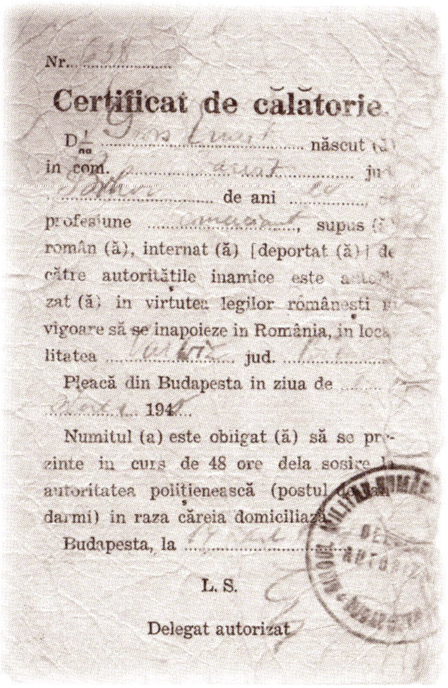

Nr. 638

Certificat de călătorie.

D[l/na] ... născut (ă) in com. ... jud. ... de ani ..., de profesiune ..., supus (ă) român (ă), internat (ă) [deportat (ă)] de către autoritățile inamice este autorizat (ă) in virtutea legilor românești in vigoare să se inapoieze in România, in localitatea ... jud. ...

Pleacă din Budapesta in ziua de ... 194..

Numitul (a) este obiigat (ă) să se prezinte in curs de 48 ore dela sosire la autoritatea poliţienească (postul de jandarmi) in raza căreia domiciliază.

Budapesta, la ...

L. S.

Delegat autorizat

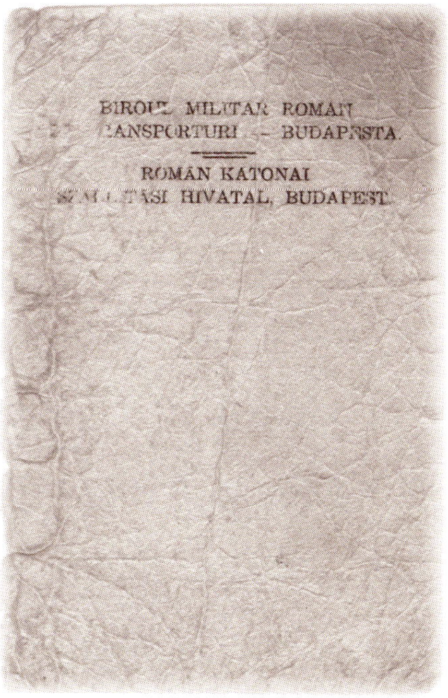

BIROUL MILITAR ROMAN
...ANSPORTURI — BUDAPESTA.

ROMÁN KATONAI
...ÁLLÍTÁSI HIVATAL, BUDAPEST.

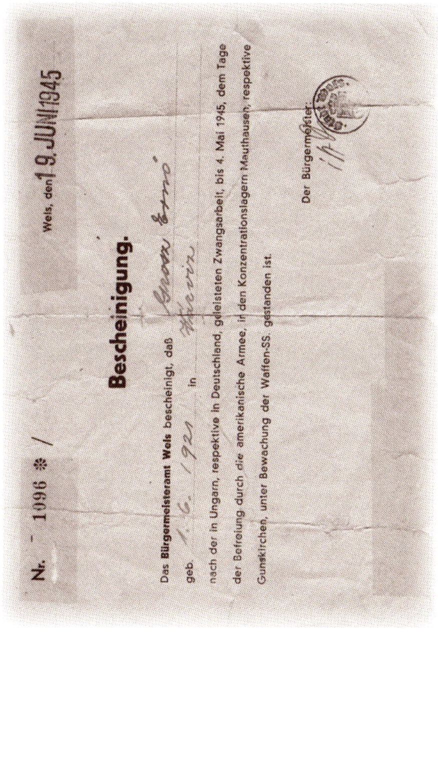

Nr. – 1096 * /

Wels, den 19. JUNI 1945

Bescheinigung.

Das **Bürgermeisteramt Wels** bescheinigt, daß Gross Ernö geb. 1. 6. 1921 in ... nach der in Ungarn, respektive in Deutschland, geleisteten Zwangsarbeit, bis 4. Mai 1945, dem Tage der Befreiung durch die amerikanische Armee, in den Konzentrationslagern Mauthausen respektive Gunskirchen, unter Bewachung der Waffen-SS. gestanden ist.

Der Bürgermeister:

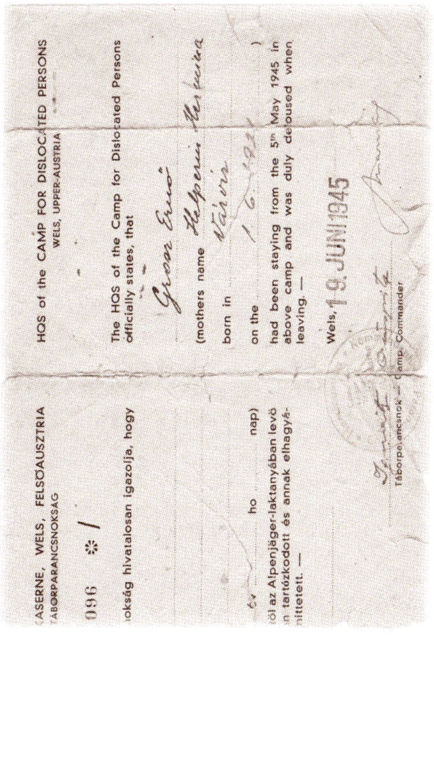

...KASERNE, WELS, FELSOAUSZTRIA
TÁBORPARANCSNOKSÁG

...096 * /

...nokság hivatalosan igazolja, hogy

...év ... hó ... nap)

...ól az Alpenjäger-laktanyában levő ...n tartózkodott és annak elhagyá...mittetett. —

Táborparancsnok — Camp Commander

HQS of the CAMP FOR DISLOCATED PERSONS
WELS, UPPER-AUSTRIA

The HQS of the Camp for Dislocated Persons officially states, that Gross Ernö (mothers name Halperin ...) born in ... on the 1. 6. 1921 had been staying from the 5th May 1945 in above camp and was duly deloused when leaving. —

Wels, 19. JUNI 1945

Táborparancsnok — Camp Commander

Names of Martyrs and Survivors from Şimleul-Silvaniei March 4,1998

This list contains the names of those who lived in my hometown Şimleul-Silvaniei (Szilagy-Somlyo) in 1940-1944. The city's Jewish Community was brutally destroyed by the Hungarian-German allies. First in 1942-1943, many Jewish men between the ages of twenty to fifty were drafted into forced labor, and gradually 90% were massacred. In the city, Jewish children, their mothers, elders, and the sick remained.

In 1944, armed soldiers forced all Jews into a ghetto in Chehul-Silvaniei (Somlyo-Chehi). The ghetto liquidation/ deportation began early Saturday, May 27, 1944, erev Shavuot. The first transport arrived in Auschwitz daybreak Friday, June 2, 1944. By miracle or fate, I Elly Gross, born Elly Berkovits survived.

In memory of the Martyrs, I will attempt to list their names, to be entered in the State Museum's Register, Auschwitz-I, Poland, and also at the registries of Yad Vashem, Israel, and the United States Holocaust Memorial Museum, Washington, D.C. Those who helped prepare this list are: Feiger Mendi, Adler-Jozsef Rachel, Jozsef Miki, Grunbaum-Jaari Eva, Moskovits-Selka Eta, and Hensel Miku.

Since 1944, fifty-four years have passed. Some first names and exact ages we do not remember; however, we know approximate ages. In 1944, we were children. A few of us are still alive. Most survivors have passed away due to their injuries suffered during the storm which swept Europe, the Holocaust. The Hungarians were overzealous to hand over every Jew to their allies, the German Nazis.

On arrival at Auschwitz-II/Birkenau, those who Dr. Mengele selected to the left were sent to gas chambers. Those who Dr. Mengele sent to the right had temporary survival. Many families had one member who perished in the Forced Labor Camps, on the March to or on the return from the Russian Front.

For family names marked ** UNKNOWN,** we know that they lived in our hometown and were deported. But we do not know their individual names.

Today no Jews live in the city of Şimleul-Silvaniei.

In Memorium

ADLER MARTON 48 YEARS OLD, SENT TO THE LEFT
ADLER'S WIFE, FEIGER EVA 39 YEARS OLD, SENT TO THE LEFT
ADLER RACHEL 19 YEARS OLD, SURVIVED
ADLER BABI 17 YEARS OLD, SURVIVED
ADLER CALI 16 YEARS OLD, SENT TO THE LEFT
ADLER SULAMITH 13 YEARS OLD, SURVIVED
ADLER JASZI 8 YEARS OLD, SENT TO THE LEFT
ADLER MOISU 4 YEARS OLD, SENT TO THE LEFT

ADLER ZALMEN-LEIB 50 YEARS OLD, SENT TO THE LEFT
ADLER ZALMA'S WIFE 48 YEARS OLD, SENT TO THE LEFT
ADLER ZALMA'S SIX CHILDREN BETWEEN AGES 10-16, ALL SENT TO THE LEFT
ADLER PERU about 19 YEARS OLD, SENT TO THE LEFT
ADLER PERU'S HUSBAND 21 YEARS OLD AND THEIR SON BORN WHILE IN THE CATTLE CAR, ALL SENT TO THE LEFT

APFELBAUM JENO ** UNKNOWN **
APFELBAUM JENO'S WIFE AND FAMILY ** UNKNOWN **

ARON LAZAR ABOUT 55 YEARS OLD, SENT TO THE LEFT
ARON LAZAR'S WIFE ABOUT 53 YEARS OLD, SENT TO THE LEFT
ARON ILONKA ABOUT 22 YEARS OLD, SURVIVED
ARON MANCI ABOUT 18 YEARS OLD, SURVIVED
ARON ARTHUR ABOUT 30 YEARS OLD, NOT SURVIVED
ARON IGNAC ABOUT 25 YEARS OLD, NOT SURVIVED
ARON OTTO ABOUT 22 YRS OLD, SURVIVED

ADLER JENO 52 YEARS OLD, SENT TO THE LEFT
ADLER'S WIFE, FEIGER CHANA 50 YEARS OLD, SENT TO THE LEFT
ADLER BABI 17 YEARS OLD, SURVIVED
ADLER JASZI 19 YEARS OLD, SURVIVED

BERGER LAJOS ABOUT 75 YEARS OLD, SENT TO THE LEFT
BERGER LAJOS'S WIFE ABOUT 70 YEARS OLD, SENT TO THE LEFT

BLAU SANDOR ABOUT 50 YEARS OLD, NOT SURVIVED
BLAU SANDOR'S WIFE, ESZTER ABOUT 45 YEARS OLD, NOT SURVIVED
BLAU SANDOR'S SEVEN SONS, HENRIK, SIMON, BUMI, ZOLI, MOSHE, MATI, JOSZI BETWEEN AGES 4, 6, 7, 8, 10, 12, 14, ALL SENT TO THE LEFT

BLAU SIMON ABOUT 35 YEARS OLD, NOT SURVIVED
BLAU SIMON'S WIFE ABOUT 34 YEARS OLD, NOT SURVIVED
BLAU SIMON'S THREE SMALL CHILDREN, SENT TO THE LEFT

BRULL SAMU ABOUT 70 YEARS OLD, SENT TO THE LEFT
BRULL SAMU'S WIFE ABOUT 65 YEARS OLD, SENT TO THE LEFT
BRULL'S DAUGHTER ABOUT 35 YEARS OLD, NOT SURVIVED
BRULL'S SON ABOUT 30 YEARS OLD, NOT SURVIVED

BURKOS JESAE ABOUT 62 YEARS OLD, SENT TO THE LEFT
BURKOS JESAE'S WIFE ABOUT 61 YEARS OLD, SENT TO THE LEFT
BURKOS ICU ABOUT 32 YEARS OLD, NOT SURVIVED
BURKOS SRULI ABOUT 20 YEARS OLD, SURVIVED
BURKOS REUVEN ABOUT 33 YEARS OLD, NOT SURVIVED
BURKOS REUVEN'S WIFE, STEINER ABOUT 30 YEARS OLD, NOT SURVIVED
BURKOS REUVEN'S TWO SMALL CHILDREN, SENT TO THE LEFT

BURKOS BUBI-IGNAC ABOUT 37 YEARS OLD, NOT SURVIVED
BURKOS BUBI'S WIFE ABOUT 35 YEARS OLD, NOT SURVIVED
BURKOS BUBI'S TWO CHILDREN 5 AND 1 YEAR OLD, SENT TO THE LEFT

BROD BENCE ABOUT 60 YEARS OLD, SENT TO THE LEFT
BROD BENCE'S WIFE ABOUT 58 YEARS OLD, SENT TO THE LEFT
BROD ERZSI ABOUT 37 YEARS OLD, SURVIVED
BROD GITA ABOUT 24 YEARS OLD, SENT TO THE RIGHT, BUT DISAPPEARED
BROD MATI ABOUT 28 YEARS OLD, SURVIVED

BROD FERENC ABOUT 70 YEARS OLD, SENT TO THE LEFT
BROD FERENC'S WIFE ABOUT 66 YEARS OLD, SENT TO THE LEFT AND
BROD KATO ABOUT 35 YEARS OLD, NOT SURVIVED
BROD KATO'S HUSBAND ABOUT 36 YEARS OLD, NOT SURVIVED
BROD EVA ABOUT 22 YEARS OLD, NOT SURVIVED
BROD IBI-ERZSIKE ABOUT 18 YEARS OLD, NOT SURVIVED
BROD FERENC'S SON ABOUT 18 YEARS OLD, SURVIVED

BRUDER KALMAN'S WIDOW ABOUT 70 YEARS OLD, SENT TO THE LEFT
BRUDER BANDI ABOUT 35 YEARS OLD, NOT SURVIVED

DR. BRUDER LASZLO ABOUT 40 YEARS OLD, NOT SURVIVED
BRUDER'S WIFE, WEISZ KATO ABOUT 36 YEARS OLD, NOT SURVIVED
BRUDER LASZLO'S SON ABOUT 15 YEARS OLD, SENT TO THE LEFT

BERKOVITS IZSO ABOUT 39 YEARS OLD, NOT SURVIVED

BERKOVITS IMRE-OCSI 12 YEARS OLD, SENT TO THE LEFT
BERKOVITS' WIFE, HENSEL IRMA ABOUT 37 YEARS OLD, SURVIVED
BERKOVITS CUNI 15 YEARS OLD, IN BIRKENAU GOT SICK AND KILLED

BERNAT ABRAHAM-NATHAN ABOUT 35 YEARS OLD, SURVIVED
BERNAT ABRAHAM'S WIFE ABOUT 33 OLD, NOT SURVIVED
BERNAT ABRAHM'S, 2 YOUNG GIRLS AND 2 BOYS, SENT TO THE LEFT

BERGER ARMIN ABOUT 35 YEARS OLD, NOT SURVIVED
BERGER ARMIN'S WIFE ABOUT 33 YEARS OLD, SENT TO THE LEFT
BERGER ARMIN'S 3 DAUGHTER'S 1, 3, AND 5 YEARS OLD, SENT TO THE LEFT

BERKOVITS JENO-EUGEN 38 YEARS OLD, NOT SURVIVED
BERKOVITS ADALBERT 5 YEARS OLD, SENT TO THE LEFT
BERKOVITS' WIFE, FARKAS IRINA 37 YEARS OLD, SENT TO THE LEFT
BERKOVITS ELLY 15 YEARS OLD, SURVIVED

DR. BERGL SANDOR ABOUT 50 YEARS OLD, NOT SURVIVED
DR. BERGL SANDOR'S WIFE ABOUT 50 YEARS OLD, NOT SURVIVED
BERGL GABI ABOUT 20 YEARS OLD, NOT SURVIVED
BERGL LILI ABOUT 18 YEARS OLD, SURVIVED
BERGL'S STEP SON, KELLER PISTI ABOUT 24 YEARS OLD, SURVIVED

BROD BERNAT ABOUT 66 YEARS OLD, SENT TO THE LEFT
BROD BERNAT'S WIFE ABOUT 64 YEARS OLD, SENT TO THE LEFT
BROD BERNAT'S SON ABOUT 30 YEARS OLD, NOT SURVIVED

BRULL GYULA ABOUT 60 YEARS OLD, SENT TO THE LEFT
BRULL GYULA'S WIFE ABOUT 55 YEARS OLD, SENT TO THE LEFT

BLAU ALBERT ABOUT 61 YEARS OLD, SENT TO THE LEFT
BLAU ALBERT'S DAUGHTER NAME ??? ABOUT 30 YEARS OLD, NOT SURVIVED
BLAU ANUS ABOUT 35 YEARS OLD, NOT SURVIVED

BERKOVITS ABOUT 65 YEARS OLD, SENT TO THE LEFT
BERKOVITS' WIFE ABOUT 60 YEARS OLD, SENT TO THE LEFT
BERKOVITS' SON ABOUT 34 YEARS OLD, NOT SURVIVED

BRAUN LAJOS' WIDOW ABOUT 76 YEARS OLD, SENT TO THE LEFT

BRAUN JENO ABOUT 35 YEARS OLD, NOT SURVIVED
BRAUN JENO'S WIFE ABOUT 33 YEARS OLD, NOT SURVIVED
BRAUN JENO'S TWO YOUNG SON'S, SENT TO THE LEFT

BASCH MARTON ABOUT 28 YEARS OLD, SURVIVED
BASCH MARTON'S WIFE ABOUT 26 YEARS OLD, NOT SURVIVED
BASCH MARTON'S FOUR SMALL CHILDREN, SENT TO THE LEFT

BASCH JOSZEF ABOUT 65 YEARS OLD, SENT TO THE LEFT
BASCH JOSZEF'S WIFE ABOUT 63 YEARS OLD, SENT TO THE LEFT
BASCH'S DAUGHTER, HAVI ABOUT 21 YEARS OLD, NOT SURVIVED
BASCH'S SON, AHARON ABOUT 24 YEARS OLD, SURVIVED
BASCH'S SON, ARI-LIEB ABOUT 26 YEARS OLD, SURVIVED
BASCH'S DAUGHTER, ZELDA ABOUT 19 YEARS OLD, SURVIVED

BARANY ABOUT 50 YEARS OLD, NOT SURVIVED
BARANY'S WIFE ABOUT 50 YEARS OLD, SENT TO THE LEFT
BARANY'S TWO DAUGHTERS ABOUT 16 AND 18 YEARS OLD, NOT SURVIVED
BARANY'S THREE SONS ABOUT 20 AND 22 OLD, NOT SURVIVED
BARANY'S SON, ERNO ABOUT 24 YEARS OLD, SURVIVED

BERGER JICCHAK-AJZIK ABOUT 52 YEARS OLD, NOT SURVIVED
BERGER'S WIFE, WEISZBERG RACHEL ABOUT 51 YEARS OLD, NOT SURVIVED
BERGER DOV-JEHUDA ABOUT 26, HIS WIVE ABOUT 24 YEARS OLD, AND
BERGER DOV-JEHUDA'S BABY, SENT TO THE LEFT
BERGER LEA ABOUT 24 YEARS OLD, NOT SURVIVED
BERGER ELIEZER 16 YEARS OLD, NOT SURVIVED
BERGER ESZTER 13 YEARS OLD, SENT TO THE LEFT
BERGER SAMUEL ABOUT 22 YEARS OLD, SURVIVED
BERGER ZEEV 20 YEARS OLD, SURVIVED
BERGER EVA 18 YEARS OLD, SURVIVED
DR. BENEDEK JOZSEF ABOUT 48 YEARS OLD, SURVIVED
BENEDEK MARGIT ABOUT 45 YEARS OLD, NOT SURVIVED
BENEDEK MARTHA ABOUT 19 YEARS OLD, NOT SURVIVED
BENEDEK OCSI 15 YEARS OLD RETURNED WITH ADVANCED TUBERCULOSIS
HE LIVED A FEW MONTHS AND DIED IN 1945

BRULL KALMAN ABOUT 75 YEARS OLD, SENT TO THE LEFT
BRULL KALMAN'S WIFE ABOUT 70 YEARS OLD, SENT TO THE LEFT
BRULL KALMAN'S SON AND DAUGHTER AND THEIR SPOUSES, NOT SURVIVED

BRULL SANDOR ABOUT 61 YEARS OLD, SENT TO THE LEFT
BRULL SANDOR'S WIFE ABOUT 56 YEARS OLD, SENT TO THE LEFT
BRULL'S TWO DAUGHTERS ABOUT 20 AND 18 YEARS OLD, NOT SURVIVED
BRULL'S SONS ABOUT 28 AND 25 YEARS OLD, NOT SURVIVED

BRACH ABOUT 37 YEARS OLD, SURVIVED
BRACH'S WIFE ABOUT 36 YEARS OLD, NOT SURVIVED
BRACH'S THREE YOUNG CHILDREN ??? YEARS OLD, SENT TO THE LEFT

BRAUN GABOR ABOUT 40 YEARS OLD, NOT SURVIVED
BRAUN GABOR'S WIFE, EVA ABOUT 38 YEARS OLD, NOT SURVIVED

CSANADI'S WIDOW ABOUT 75 YEARS OLD, SENT TO THE LEFT
CSANADI'S DAUGHTER ABOUT 45 YEARS OLD, NOT SURVIVED

CSENGERI MIHALY-CHAIM ABOUT 62 YEARS OLD, SENT TO THE LEFT
CSENGERI'S WIFE, LOWINGER ROZSI 52 YEARS OLD, SENT TO THE LEFT
CSENGERI GEZA 25 YEARS OLD, NOT SURVIVED
CSENGERI MARTON 14 YEARS OLD, SENT TO THE LEFT
CSENGERI IMRE-JEHUDA ABOUT 23 YEARS OLD, SURVIVED
CSENGERI FERENC-ZVI ABOUT 30 YEARS OLD, SURVIVED
CSENGERI'S WIFE, ENGEL ROZSI TWIN'S MOTHER 29 YEARS OLD, SURVIVED
CSENGERI FERENC'S TWIN DAUGHTERS LIA & JUDIT 7 YEARS OLD, SURVIVED

CZEIZLER BERNAT ABOUT 64 YEARS OLD, SENT TO THE LEFT
CZEIZLER BERNAT'S WIFE ABOUT 62 YEARS OLD, SENT TO THE LEFT

CZEIZLER ABOUT 50 YEARS OLD, NOT SURVIVED
CZEIZLER'S WIFE ABOUT 46 YEARS OLD, NOT SURVIVED
CZEIZLER'S SON ABOUT 24 YEARS OLD, NOT SURVIVED
CZEIZLER'S DAUGHTER ABOUT 20 YEARS OLD, NOT SURVIVED

CSENGERI BERTALAN-DOV ABOUT 52 YEARS OLD, SENT TO THE LEFT
CSENGERI BERTALAN-DOV'S WIFE ABOUT 50 YEARS OLD, SENT TO THE LEFT
CSENGERI SULEM ABOUT 27 YEARS OLD, NOT SURVIVED
CSENGERI HAINAL ABOUT 35 YEARS OLD, NOT SURVIVED
CSENGERI HAINAL'S HUSBAND ABOUT 38 YEARS OLD, ** UNKNOWN **
CSENGERI HAINAL'S SMALL CHILDREN ??? YEARS OLD, SENT TO THE LEFT

DAVID JOZSEF-MOSHE 54 YEARS OLD, NOT SURVIVED
DAVID'S WIFE, SCHWATZ CHAJA 52 YEARS OLD, SENT TO THE LEFT
DAVID AVRAHAM-ADOLF 24 YEARS OLD, NOT SURVIVED
DAVID RELLA-RIVKA 21 YEARS OLD, NOT SURVIVED
DAVID GIZI ABOUT 35 YEARS OLD, NOT SURVIVED
DAVID GIZI'S DAUGHTER EVA 10 YEARS OLD, SENT TO THE LEFT
DAVID GIZI'S SON GYURI 5 YEARS OLD, SENT TO THE LEFT
DAVID GIZI'S HUSBAND ABOUT 38 YEARS OLD, SURVIVED ** UNKNOWN **

DAVIDOVITS ABOUT 45 YEARS OLD, NOT SURVIVED
DAVIDOVITS'S WIFE ABOUT 40 YEARS OLD, NOT SURVIVED

DAJEN LAWFER'S WIDOW ABOUT 68 YEARS OLD, SENT TO THE LEFT
D. LAUFER MIRIAM 28, HER HUSBAND ABOUT 34 YEARS OLD, NOT SURVIVED, DAJEN LAUFER MIRIAM'S, FOUR YOUNG CHILDREN, SENT TO THE LEFT
D. LAUFER'S DAUGHTER, HER HUSBAND AND TWO CHILDREN, NOT SURVIVED
D. LAUFER SULEM ABOUT 20 YEARS OLD, SURVIVED
D. LAUFER SIJE ABOUT 30 YEARS OLD, SURVIVED

EHRENREICH MOZES-MOSHE ABOUT 50 YEARS OLD, SENT TO THE LEFT
EHRENREICH MOZES' WIFE ABOUT 49 YEARS OLD, SENT TO THE LEFT
EHRENREICH SON ABOUT 17 YEARS OLD, NOT SURVIVED
EHRENREICH HINDU ABOUT 25 YEARS OLD AND HER HUSBAND, NOT SURVIVED
EHRENREICH CIVIA ABOUT 22 YEARS OLD AND HER HUSBAND, NOT SURVIVED
EHRENREICH HINDU AND CIVIA'S FIVE SMALL CHILDREN, SENT TO THE LEFT
EHRENREICH LIE ABOUT 20 YEARS OLD, NOT SURVIVED
EHRENREICH JANKU ABOUT 19 YEARS OLD, SURVIVED
EHRENREICH FEIGI ABOUT 18 YEARS OLD, SURVIVED & LIVED A FEW MONTHS
EHRENREICH RAIZI ABOUT 16 YEARS OLD, SURVIVED

EHRENREICH SAMUEL (SHLOMO-ZALMAN) 82 YEARS OLD, SENT TO THE LEFT
EHRENREICH SAMUEL'S WIFE 79 YEARS OLD SENT, TO THE LEFT
EHRENREICH SIMON ABOUT 40 YEARS OLD, HIS WIFE ABOUT 36 YEARS OLD
EHRENREICH SIMON'S SIX SMALL CHILDREN, SENT TO THE LEFT

EHRENREICH JEHOSUA ABOUT 36 YEARS OLD, SURVIVED (IN ROMANIA)
EHRENREICH JEHOSUA'S WIFE ABOUT 34 YEARS OLD, SURVIVED (IN ROMANIA)
EHRENREICH JEHOSUA'S 4 CHILDREN YRS OLD, SURVIVED (IN ROMANIA)

ECKSTEIN IZIDOR ABOUT 38 YEARS OLD, SURVIVED
ECKSTEIN'S WIFE, MARKOVITS MANCI ABOUT 35 YRS OLD, SENT TO THE LEFT
ECKSTEIN'S FIVE YOUNG CHILDREN 2 BOY'S 3 GIRL'S, SENT TO THE LEFT

EHRENREICH CHAIM ABOUT 39 YEARS OLD, NOT SURVIVED
EHRENREICH CHAIM'S WIFE ABOUT 36 YEARS OLD, NOT SURVIVED
EHRENREICH CHAIM'S FIVE SMALL CHILDREN, SENT TO THE LEFT

ENGEL SAMUEL-ZANVEL ABOUT 60 YEARS OLD, SENT TO THE LEFT
ENGEL'S WIFE, KLEIN BERTA ABOUT 58 YEARS OLD, SENT TO THE LEFT
ENGEL ERNO ABOUT 28 YEARS OLD, SURVIVED
ENGEL ILONKA ABOUT 21 YEARS OLD, SURVIVED
ENGEL GABI ABOUT 18 YEARS OLD, SURVIVED
ENGEL MIKSA ABOUT 30 YEARS OLD, NOT SURVIVED
ENGEL MIKSA'S WIFE GIZA ABOUT 28 YEARS OLD, NOT SURVIVED
ENGEL MIKSA'S SON ABOUT 10 YEARS OLD, SENT TO THE LEFT

ECKSTEIN JISZRAEL-HAJEM ABOUT 30 YEARS OLD, NOT SURVIVED
ECKSTEIN JISZRAEL'S WIFE ABOUT 28 YEARS OLD, NOT SURVIVED
ECKSTEIN JISZRAEL'S FOUR SMALL CHILDREN, SENT TO THE LEFT

EHRENFELD'S WIDOW ABOUT 65 YEARS OLD, SENT TO THE LEFT
EHRENFELD ILUS ABOUT 40 YEARS OLD, NOT SURVIVED

FELDHEIM SAMUEL ABOUT 55 YEARS OLD (POLICE SERGEANT), NOT SURVIVED
FELDHEIM SAMUEL'S WIFE ABOUT 53 YEARS OLD, NOT SURVIVED

FEKETE BELA ABOUT 53 YEARS OLD, NOT SURVIVED
FEKETE BELA'S WIFE ABOUT 50 YEARS OLD, NOT SURVIVED
FEKETE BELA'S SON ABOUT 26 YEARS OLD, NOT SURVIVED

FRIED MIHALY ABOUT 70 YEARS OLD, SENT TO THE LEFT
FRIED MIHALY'S WIFE ABOUT 66 YEARS OLD, SENT TO THE LEFT
FRIED MIHALY'S TWO MARRIED DAUGHTER'S, THEIR HUSBAND'S AND SMALL CHILDREN, NOT SURVIVED ??? YEARS OLD ** UNKNOWN **
FRIED MIHALY'S TWO SONS BELA AND SAMU ??? YEARS OLD, NOT SURVIVED

FENER SAJE-AKIVA ABOUT 40 YEARS OLD, SURVIVED
FENER SAJE-AKIVA'S WIFE ABOUT 38 YEARS OLD, NOT SURVIVED
FENER SAJE'S TWO SMALL CHILDREN ??? YEARS OLD, NOT SURVIVED

FRIEDMAN NANDOR ABOUT 40 YEARS, OLD NOT SURVIVED
FRIEDMAN NANDOR'S WIFE ABOUT 40 YEARS, SENT TO THE LEFT
FRIEDMAN NANDOR'S TWO SMALL CHILDREN, SENT TO THE LEFT

FRANKOVITS SANDOR ABOUT 50 YEARS OLD, SENT TO THE LEFT
FRANKOVITS SANDOR'S MOTHER ABOUT 72 YEARS OLD, SENT TO THE LEFT

FISCHMAN SANDOR ABOUT 35 YEARS OLD, SURVIVED
FISCHMAN'S WIFE,IZSAK BOSKE ABOUT 33 YEARS OLD, NOT SURVIVED
FISCHMAN TIBI ABOUT 12 YEARS OLD, SENT TO THE LEFT
FISCHMAN MARIKA ABOUT 10 YEARS OLD, SENT TO THE LEFT
FISCHMAN MARTON ??? YEARS OLD, NOT SURVIVED
FISCHMAN BELA ??? YEARS OLD, NOT SURVIVED ** AGES UNKNOWN **
FISCHMAN LAJOS ??? YEARS OLD, NOT SURVIVED ** ???? **
FISCHMAN ERNO ??? YEARS OLD, NOT SURVIVED ** ???? **

FISCHMAN FERENC ABOUT 65 YEARS OLD, SENT TO THE LEFT
FISCHMAN-HOLZER BERTA ABOUT 62 YEARS OLD, SENT TO THE LEFT
FISCHMAN MORIC ??? YEARS OLD, SURVIVED
FISCHMAN JOZSI ABOUT 38 YEARS OLD, NOT SURVIVED
FISCHMAN JOZSI'S WIVE ABOUT 36 & THREE SMALL CHILDREN, NOT SURVIVED

FRANKEL 45 YEARS OLD, NOT SURVIVED
FRANKEL'S WIFE 42 YEARS OLD, NOT SURVIVED
FRANKEL FRIMI ABOUT 12 YEARS OLD, NOT SURVIVED
FRANKEL HAINAL ABOUT 17 YEARS OLD, SURVIVED

FEIG HERMAN ABOUT 40 YEARS OLD, NOT SURVIVED
FEIG-PASZTERNAK CHANI ABOUT 38 YEARS OLD, SENT TO THE LEFT
FEIG DUVED 17 YEARS OLD, NOT SURVIVED
FEIG AIDA 15 YEARS OLD, SENT TO THE LEFT
FEIG BAILU 13 YEARS OLD, SENT TO THE LEFT
FEIG RUCI 10 YEARS OLD, SENT TO THE LEFT

FRIED DEZSO ABOUT 40 YEARS OLD, NOT SURVIVED
FRIED DEZSO'S WIFE ABOUT 37 YEARS OLD, NOT SURVIVED
FRIED DEZSO'S TWO CHILDREN ??? YEARS OLD, NOT SURVIVED

FEIBUSZ MEIR ABOUT 55 YEARS OLD, SENT TO THE LEFT
FEIBUSZ MEIR'S WIFE ABOUT 54 YEARS OLD, SENT TO THE LEFT
FEIBUSZ SARI 19 YEARS OLD, SENT TO THE LEFT
FEIBUSZ FEIGI 14 YEARS OLD, SENT TO THE LEFT
FEIBUSZ MEIR'S YOUNG SON 16 YEARS OLD, SENT TO THE LEFT
FEIBUSZ MOSHE ABOUT 20 YEARS OLD, SURVIVED

FARKAS FERENC'S WIDOW, IDA 60 YEARS OLD, SENT TO THE LEFT

FRIEDMAN JOZSEF'S WIDOW ABOUT 45 YEARS OLD, NOT SURVIVED
FREIDMAN JOZSEF'S DAUGHTER ABOUT 17 YEARS OLD, NOT SURVIVED

FARKAS IGNAC ABOUT 40 YEARS OLD, NOT SURVIVED
FARKAS IGNAC'S WIFE, WEISZ ABOUT 39 YEARS OLD, NOT SURVIVED
FARKAS BAILU ABOUT 19 YEARS OLD, SURVIVED

FRIEDMAN JENO ABOUT 39 YEARS OLD, NOT SURVIVED
FRIEDMAN JENO'S WIFE ABOUT 38 YEARS OLD, NOT SURVIVED
FRIEDMAN EVA ABOUT 14 YEARS OLD, NOT SURVIVED

FEIGER SALAMON-SLOMO 67 YEARS OLD, SENT TO THE LEFT
FEIGER'S WIFE, KRONSTEIN REZSI 58 YEARS OLD, SENT TO THE LEFT
FEIGER ROZSI ABOUT 36 YEARS OLD, SURVIVED
FEIGER FANI ABOUT 33 YEARS OLD, SURVIVED
FEIGER MENDU 29 YEARS OLD, SURVIVED
FEIGER DORI ABOUT 31 YEARS OLD, NOT SURVIVED

FEIGER A. MOZES 55 YEARS OLD, SENT TO THE LEFT
FEIGER ROZSI 48 YEARS OLD, SENT TO THE LEFT
FEIGER JASZI 20 YEARS OLD, SURVIVED
FEIGER JANKI 22 YEARS OLD, SURVIVED
FEIGER MENDI 8 YEARS OLD, SENT TO THE LEFT

FOGEL JONA ABOUT 64 YEARS OLD, SENT TO THE LEFT
FOGEL JONA'S WIFE ABOUT 63 YEARS OLD, SENT TO THE LEFT
FOGEL JONA'S SIX MARRIED CHILDREN, THEIR WIVE'S, NOT SURVIVED
FOGEL JONA'S ABOUT 15-20 GRANDCHILDREN, SENT TO THE LEFT

FELDMAN BENJAMIN-BENZION ABOUT 73 YEARS OLD, SENT TO THE LEFT
FELDMAN BENJAMIN'S WIFE ABOUT 70 YEARS OLD, SENT TO THE LEFT
FELDHAM'S SON 50, HIS WIFE 46, THEIR SON JANKI 24, DAUGHTER MALIN 24,
OTHER DAUGHTER 26, GRAND CHILDREN 6, 8, AND 10, NOT SURVIVED

FLEISHMAN HERMAN ABOUT 48 YEARS OLD, NOT SURVIVED
FLEISHMAN HERMAN'S WIFE ABOUT 45 YEARS OLD, NOT SURVIVED
FLEISHMAN ITU ABOUT 15 YEARS OLD, SENT TO THE LEFT
FLEISHMAN SONS ABOUT 13, 10 AND 8 YEARS OLD, SENT TO THE LEFT
FLEISHMAN MALKI 20 YEARS OLD, SURVIVED
FLEISHMAN MOSHE 22 YEARS OLD, SURVIVED

DR. FRIED VILMOS ABOUT 53 YEARS OLD, NOT SURVIVED
FRIED'S WIFE, FRANKOVITS ROZSI ABOUT 50 YEARS OLD, NOT SURVIVED
FRIED ZSUZSI ABOUT 18 YEARS OLD, NOT SURVIVED

FREUND CHAIM ABOUT 45 YEARS OLD, NOT SURVIVED
FREUND CHAIM'S WIFE ABOUT 44 YEARS OLD, NOT SURVIVED

FEIGER ARMIN ABOUT 36 YEARS OLD, SURVIVED
FEIGER'S WIFE, TONI ABOUT 33 YEARS OLD, NOT SURVIVED
FEIGER DAVID 8 YEARS OLD, SENT TO THE LEFT
FEIGER'S DAUGHTER 3 YEARS OLD, SENT TO THE LEFT

FINKELSTEIN ABOUT 71 YEARS OLD, SENT TO THE LEFT
FINKELSTEIN'S WIFE ABOUT 70 YEARS OLD, SENT TO THE LEFT
FINKELSTEIN'S FOUR SONS ??? YEARS OLD, THEIR SPOUSES, NOT SURVIVED,
FINKELSTEIN'S ABOUT EIGHT YOUNG GRANDCHILDREN, SENT TO THE LEFT

FRANKEL FERENC ABOUT 45 YEARS OLD, NOT SURVIVED
FRANKEL FERENC'S WIFE ABOUT 40 YEARS OLD, NOT SURVIVED
FRANKEL FERENC'S TWO CHILDREN, NOT SURVIVED

FRIEDMAN ERNO ABOUT 35 YEARS OLD, NOT SURVIVED
FRIEDMAN ERNO'S WIFE ABOUT 32 YEARS OLD, NOT SURVIVED

FRIEDMAN ERNO'S TWO CHILDREN 8 AND 10 YEARS OLD, SENT TO THE LEFT

GROSZ MENDEL ABOUT 65 YEARS OLD, NOT SURVIVED
GROSZ'S WIFE ABOUT 63 YEARS OLD, NOT SURVIVED
GROSZ NUSI 20 YEARS OLD, NOT SURVIVED
GROSZ MENDEL'S SON ABOUT 23 YEARS OLD, NOT SURVIVED
GROSZ BANDI ABOUT 26 YEARS OLD, NOT SURVIVED
GROSZ BUMI ABOUT 18 YEARS OLD, SURVIVED

GROSZ ARPAD ABOUT 44 YEARS OLD, SURVIVED
GROSZ ARPAD'S WIFE ABOUT 39 YEARS OLD, NOT SURVIVED
GROSZ'S DAUGHTER 14 YEARS OLD, NOT SURVIVED
GROSZ ARPAD'S FOUR SONS ABOUT 6-12 YEARS OLD, SENT TO THE LEFT

GRUNBAUM'S WIDOW ROZSI 54 YEARS OLD, SENT TO THE LEFT
GRUNBAUM LILI 22 YEARS OLD, NOT SURVIVED
GRUNBAUM CLARI 15 YEARS OLD, SURVIVED

GRUNBAUM MOSHE 78 YEARS OLD, SENT TO THE LEFT
GRUNBAUM CHANA 72 YEARS OLD, SENT TO THE LEFT
GRUNBAUM HILLEL 48 YEARS OLD, NOT SURVIVED
GRUNBAUM'S WIFE, GROSS SZEREN 36 YEARS OLD, NOT SURVIVED
GRUNBAUM HILLEL'S FOUR CHILDREN ??? YEARS OLD, NOT SURVIVED

GROSZMAN MENYERT ABOUT 55 YEARS OLD, NOT SURVIVED
GROSZMAN MENYERT'S WIFE ABOUT 54 YEARS OLD, NOT SURVIVED
GROSZMAN MENYERT'S DAUGHTER ABOUT 28 YEARS OLD, NOT SURVIVED
GROSZMAN LACI ABOUT 25 YEARS OLD, SURVIVED

GLUCK MOR-MOSHE ABOUT 53 YEARS OLD, NOT SURVIVED
GLUCK MOR-MOSHE'S WIFE ABOUT 50 YEARS OLD, NOT SURVIVED
GLUCK MOR-MOSHE'S TWO DAUGHTERS ABOUT 22 AND 29 YEARS OLD,
THEIR SPOUSES AND SMALL CHILDREN, NOT SURVIVED
GLUCK ZOLI ABOUT 28 YEARS OLD, ** UNKNOWN **

GROSZ SANDOR ABOUT 50 YEARS OLD, NOT SURVIVED
GROSZ SANDOR'S WIFE ABOUT 48 YEARS OLD, NOT SURVIVED
GROSZ SANDOR'S SON ABOUT 26 YEARS OLD, NOT SURVIVED

GLUCK WILMOS ABOUT 35 YEARS OLD, NOT SURVIVED
GLUCK CORNEL ABOUT 33 YEARS OLD, NOT SURVIVED
GLUCK WILMOS'S THREE SONS ??? YEARS OLD, NOT SURVIVED ** UNKNOWN **

GRUNSTEIN SZIMCHE ABOUT 40 YEARS OLD, NOT SURVIVED
GRUNSTEIN SZIMCHE'S WIFE ABOUT 38 YEARS OLD, NOT SURVIVED
GRUNSTEIN SZIMCHE'S TWO CHILDREN, SENT TO THE LEFT
GLUCK ABRAHAM ABOUT 70 YEARS OLD, SENT TO THE LEFT
GLUCK ABRAHAM'S WIFE ABOUT 66 YEARS OLD, SENT TO THE LEFT
GLUCK GEZA ABOUT 26 YEARS OLD, NOT SURVIVED

GRUNBAUM FERENC 46 YEARS OLD, NOT SURVIVED
GRUNBAUM'S WIFE, KRAFT SARA 40 YEARS OLD, NOT SURVIVED
GRUNBAUM LALI-PUFI 22 YEARS OLD, SURVIVED SICK, LIVED A FEW MONTHS
GRUNBAUM EVA 18 YEARS OLD, SURVIVED

GOLDBERGER SANDOR ABOUT 60 YEARS OLD, SENT TO THE LEFT
GOLDBERGER SANDOR'S ABOUT WIFE 58 YEARS OLD, SENT TO THE LEFT

GOLDGLANCZ MOR ABOUT 59 YEARS OLD, SENT TO THE LEFT
GOLDGLANCZ MOR'S WIFE ABOUT 57 YEARS OLD, SENT TO THE LEFT
GOLDGLANCZ KATO 20 YEARS OLD, NOT SURVIVED

DR. GAL LASZLO ABOUT 51 YEARS OLD, SURVIVED, BUT DISAPPEARED
DR. GAL'S WIFE ABOUT 50 YEARS OLD, NOT SURVIVED

GIDALY JOSZEF ABOUT 61 YEARS OLD, SENT TO THE LEFT
GIDALY JOSZEF'S ABOUT WIFE 55 YEARS OLD, SENT TO THE LEFT
GIDALY LACI ABOUT 28 YEARS OLD, NOT SURVIVED
GIDALY SANYI ABOUT 33 YEARS OLD, SURVIVED
GIDALY MIKLOS ABOUT 38 YEARS OLD, SURVIVED
GIDALY MIKLOS' WIFE, SMUCK ABOUT 34 YEARS OLD, NOT SURVIVED
GIDALY MIKLOS' TWO SMALL CHILDREN, SENT TO THE LEFT
GIDALY IMRE ABOUT 38 YEARS OLD, SURVIVED
GIDALY IMRE'S WIFE ABOUT 35 YEARS OLD, NOT SURVIVED
GIDALY IMRE'S 10 YEARS OLD CHILD, SENT TO THE LEFT

GLUCK SALAMON ABOUT 58 YEARS OLD, SENT TO THE LEFT
GLUCK SALAMON'S WIFE ABOUT 55 YEARS OLD, SENT TO THE LEFT
GLUCK RUDI ABOUT 22 YEARS OLD, NOT SURVIVED
GLUCK SARI ABOUT 30 YEARS OLD, NOT SURVIVED
GLUCK ROZSI ABOUT 19 YEARS OLD, SURVIVED

GLUCK'S WIDOW ABOUT 60 YEARS OLD, SENT TO THE LEFT
GLUCK'S DAUGHTER ABOUT 32 YEARS OLD, NOT SURVIVED
GLUCK LIPU ABOUT 36 YEARS OLD, NOT SURVIVED
GLUCK WILMOS ABOUT 38 YEARS OLD, NOT SURVIVED

GRUNFELD ALBERT ABOUT 37 YEARS OLD, NOT SURVIVED
GRUNFELD ALBERT'S WIFE ABOUT 35 YEARS OLD, SENT TO THE LEFT
GRUNFELD ALBERT'S TWO CHILDREN ??? YEARS OLD, SENT TO THE LEFT

GLUCK MIKLOS ABOUT 29 YEARS OLD, NOT SURVIVED
GLUCK'S WIFE, STEINBERG IRMA ABOUT 27 YEARS OLD, NOT SURVIVED
GLUCK'S DAUGHTER EVA, ABOUT SIX YEARS OLD, SENT TO THE LEFT

GROSZ JOSZEF-SIJE ABOUT 40 YEARS OLD, NOT SURVIVED
GROSZ JOSZEF-SIJE'S WIFE ABOUT 36 YEARS OLD, SENT TO THE LEFT
GROSZ JOSZEF'S DAUGHTERS 13 AND 10 YEARS OLD, SENT TO THE LEFT

GUNZLER WILMOS ABOUT 65 YEARS OLD, SENT TO THE LEFT
GUNZLER WILMOS'S WIFE ABOUT 59 YEARS OLD, SENT TO THE LEFT

GROSZ ABOUT 40 YEARS OLD, NOT SURVIVED
GROSZ'S WIFE ROSENBERG ELLA ABOUT 38 YEARS OLD, NOT SURVIVED
GROSZ'S THREE YOUNG CHILDREN ABOUT 7-14 YEARS OLD, SENT TO THE LEFT

GRUNBERGER ABOUT 70 YEARS OLD, SENT TO THE LEFT
GRUNBERGER'S WIFE ABOUT 61 YEARS OLD, SENT TO THE LEFT

GRUNSTEIN ABOUT 55 YEARS OLD, SENT TO THE LEFT
GRUNSTEIN'S WIFE ABOUT 53 YEARS OLD, SENT TO THE LEFT
GRUNSTEIN JIDLE 18 YEARS OLD, NOT SURVIVED
GRUNSTEIN ICI-HAIEM 16 YEARS OLD, NOT SURVIVED
GRUNSTEIN MARTON 20 YEARS OLD, SURVIVED
GRUNSTEIN ZITA 19 YEARS OLD, SURVIVED
GRUNSTEIN EVA 17 YEARS OLD, SURVIVED

HOLCZER ABOUT 60 YEARS OLD, SENT TO THE LEFT
HOLCZER'S WIFE ABOUT 58 YEARS OLD, SENT TO THE LEFT
HOLCZER'S THREE CHILDREN ??? YEARS OLD, THEIR SPOUSES ??? YEARS OLD,
INCLUDING THEIR CHILDREN ??? YEARS OLD, NOT SURVIVED

HERSKOVITS IGNAC ABOUT 40 YEARS OLD, SURVIVED
HERSKOVITS IGNAC'S WIFE ABOUT 38 YEARS OLD, NOT SURVIVED
HERSKOVITS IGNAC'S TWO CHILDREN, SENT TO THE LEFT

HEGYESI JENO ABOUT 56 YEARS OLD, NOT SURVIVED
HEGYESI JENO'S WIFE ABOUT 54 YEARS OLD, NOT SURVIVED
HEGYESI BANDI ABOUT 20 YEARS OLD, NOT SURVIVED

HELPERIN GIZELLA 56 YRS OLD TO ESCAPE DEPORTATION POISONED HERSELF
HELPERIN ERNO 28 YEARS OLD TO ESCAPE DEPORTATION POISONED HIMSELF

HENSEL'S WIDOW, MARKOVITS ESTER 58 YEARS OLD, SENT TO THE LEFT
HENSEL ZALMI ABOUT 24 YEARS OLD, SURVIVED
HENSEL MIKU ABOUT 26 YEARS OLD, SURVIVED
HENSEL'S DAUGHTER, UNGAR ELLA ABOUT 34 YEARS OLD, SENT TO THE LEFT
H. (UNGAR ELLA'S) DAUGHTER, KATY ABOUT 10 YRS OLD, SENT TO THE LEFT
H. (UNGAR ELLA'S) SON, BERL ABOUT 7 YEARS OLD, SENT TO THE LEFT
HENSEL ELLA'S HUSBAND, UNGAR MORIC ABOUT 39 YEARS OLD, SURVIVED
HIRSHFELD HILLEL ABOUT 40 YEARS OLD, NOT SURVIVED
HIRSHFELD HILLEL'S WIFE ABOUT 39 YEARS OLD, NOT SURVIVED
HIRSHFELD RIVU ABOUT 19 YEARS OLD, SURVIVED
HIRSHFELD MAJU ABOUT 17 YEARS OLD, SURVIVED
HIRSHFELD FEIGI ABOUT 22 YEARS OLD, NOT SURVIVED
HIRSHFELD'S SONS NUTY ABOUT 20 AND SMILU ABOUT 24, NOT SURVIVED
HIRSHFELD'S TWO STEPDAUGHTERS ??? YEARS OLD, NOT SURVIVED

HEIMLICH NAFTALI ABOUT 55 YEARS OLD, NOT SURVIVED
HEIMLICH NAFTALI'S WIFE ABOUT 52 YEARS OLD, NOT SURVIVED

HEIMLICH ETI 25 YRS OLD HER HUSBAND & 3 CHILDREN, SENT TO THE LEFT
HEIMLICH JICHAG 30 YRS OLD HIS WIFE & 5 CHILDREN, SENT TO THE LEFT
HIRSH ALADAR ABOUT 40 YEARS OLD, SURVIVED
HIRSH-HENDLER ROZSI ABOUT 36 YEARS OLD, NOT SURVIVED
HIRSH'S 2 DAUGHTERS 10, 12 ONE BOY 8 YRS OLD, SENT TO THE LEFT

HANDLER ABOUT 52 YEARS OLD, NOT SURVIVED
HANDLER'S WIFE ABOUT 48 YEARS OLD, NOT SURVIVED
HANDLER ERZSI ABOUT 24 YEARS OLD, SURVIVED

HEIMLICH SANDOR ABOUT 70 YEARS OLD, SENT TO THE LEFT
HEIMLICH SANDOR'S WIFE ABOUT 67 YEARS OLD, SENT TO THE LEFT

HEIMLICH MOSHE-MORDECHAI ABOUT 58 YEARS OLD, NOT SURVIVED
HEIMLICH MOSHE'S WIFE ABOUT 57 YEARS OLD, NOT SURVIVED
HEIMLICH BABA 19 YEARS OLD, SURVIVED
HEIMLICH CHAILU 17 YEARS OLD, SURVIVED
HEIMLICH MOSHE'S TWO SONS AGES 14 AND 20 NOT SURVIVED

HEIMLICH SIJE ABOUT 50 YEARS OLD, NOT SURVIVE
HEIMLICH SIJE'S WIFE ABOUT 45 YEARS OLD, SURVIVED
HEIMLICH ZISZU ABOUT 18 YEARS OLD, SURVIVED
HEIMLICH BICU ABOUT 22 YEARS OLD, SURVIVED
HEIMLICH DUVED ABOUT 19 YEARS OLD, SURVIVED
HEIMLICH HAVI ABOUT 16 YEARS OLD, NOT SURVIVED

HERSKOVITS ABOUT 40 YEARS OLD, NOT SURVIVED
HERSKOVITS'S WIFE ABOUT 35 YEARS OLD, NOT SURVIVED

HERSCHLI JAKAB ABOUT 65 YEARS OLD, SENT TO THE LEFT
HERSCHLI JAKAB'S WIFE ABOUT 60 YEARS OLD, SENT TO THE LEFT
HERSCHLI'S SON AND TWO DAUGHTERS, NOT SURVIVED
HERSCHLI'S MARRIED SON'S & DAUGHTERS' SPOUSES, NOT SURVIVED
HERSCHLI'S GRANDDAUGHTER ZIZI ABOUT 18 YEARS OLD, SURVIVED
HERSCHLI'S OTHER GRANDCHILDREN ??? YEARS OLD, NOT SURVIVED

HERSCHLI SANDOR ABOUT 38 YEARS OLD, SENT TO THE LEFT
HERSCHLI BOZSI ABOUT 37 YRS OLD, SENT TO THE LEFT
HERSCHLI SANDOR'S TWO YOUNG CHILDREN, SENT TO THE LEFT

HIRSCH SALAMON-ZALMI ABOUT 55 YEARS OLD, SENT TO THE LEFT
HIRSCH SALALMON'S WIFE ABOUT 54 YEARS OLD, SENT TO THE LEFT
HIRSCH SALALMON'S TWO MARRIED DAUGHTERS 24, 22 YEARS OLD, ALSO HIRSCH DAUGHTERS' HUSBANDS AND CHILDREN, NOT SURVIVED
HIRSCH SON 28 YEARS OLD, HIS WIFE 2 CHILDREN, NOT SURVIVED

HIRSCH ZALI'S WIDOW ABOUT 58 YEARS OLD, SENT TO THE LEFT

HIRSCH ODON ABOUT 60 YEARS OLD, SENT TO THE LEFT
HIRSCH ODON'S WIFE ABOUT 55 YEARS OLD, SENT TO THE LEFT

HIRSCH CLARI ABOUT 30 YEARS OLD, NOT SURVIVED
HANDLER SMAJE ABOUT 40 YEARS OLD, NOT SURVIVED
HANDLER SMAJE'S WIFE ABOUT 38 YEARS OLD, NOT SURVIVED
HANDLER SMAJE'S FOUR YOUNG CHILDREN, SENT TO THE LEFT

INDIG ABOUT 65 YEARS OLD, SENT TO THE LEFT
INDIG'S WIFE ABOUT 63 YEARS, OLD SENT TO THE LEFT
INDIG'S TWO DAUGHTERS 40 AND 38 YEARS OLD, SENT TO THE LEFT

IZSAK JAKAB ABOUT 59 YEARS OLD, SENT TO THE LEFT
IZSAK JAKAB'S WIFE ABOUT 55 YEARS OLD, SENT TO THE LEFT
IZSAK IBI ABOUT 16 YEARS OLD, NOT SURVIVED
IZSAK PASTS ABOUT 18 YEARS OLD, SURVIVED
IZSAK SMILU SON ABOUT 22 YEARS OLD, SURVIVED
IZSAK DEZSO 20 YEARS OLD, SURVIVED

IZSAK FERENC ABOUT 50 YEARS OLD, SENT TO THE LEFT
IZSAK FERENC'S WIFE ABOUT 47 YEARS OLD, SENT TO THE LEFT
IZSAK JOZSI ABOUT 24 YEARS OLD, SURVIVED
IZSAK ZOLI ABOUT 19 YEARS OLD, NOT SURVIVED
IZSAK LILI 17 YEARS OLD, SURVIVED

IZSAK JAKAB ABOUT 40 YEARS OLD, NOT SURVIVED
IZSAK JAKAB'S WIFE ABOUT 38 YEARS OLD, NOT SURVIVED
IZSAK JAKAB'S TWO SONS ABOUT 17 AND 15 YEARS OLD, NOT SURVIVED

IZSAK ALBERT ABOUT 39 YEARS OLD, NOT SURVIVED
IZSAK ALBERT'S WIFE ABOUT 35 YEARS OLD, NOT SURVIVED
IZSAK ALBERT'S FIVE SMALL CHILDREN, SENT TO THE LEFT

JUROVITS ABOUT 42 YEARS OLD, NOT SURVIVED
JUROVITS'S WIFE ABOUT 37 YEARS OLD, NOT SURVIVED
JUROVITS'S SON MAYER ABOUT 17 YEARS OLD, NOT SURVIVED
JUROVITS'S SON ANDOR ABOUT 15 YEARS OLD, NOT SURVIVED

JAMBERGER NANDOR-NAFTALI ABOUT 50 YEARS OLD, NOT SURVIVED
JAMBERGER SZEREN-SLOVA ABOUT 48 YEARS OLD, NOT SURVIVED
JAMBERGER LILI ABOUT 27 YEARS OLD, NOT SURVIVED
J. LILI'S HUSBAND, MARKOVITS SANYI ABOUT 30 YEARS OLD, SURVIVED
JAMBERGER LILI'S SON ARI ABOUT 6 YEARS OLD, SENT TO THE LEFT
JAMBERGER LILI'S DAUGHTER ITUKA ABOUT 4 YEARS OLD, SENT TO THE LEFT
JAMBERGER RELLI-RACHEL ABOUT 19 YEARS OLD, SURVIVED
JAMBERGER STEFI ABOUT 21 YEARS OLD, SURVIVED
JAMBERGER EDITH ABOUT 23 YEARS OLD, SURVIVED

JAKAB'S WIDOW ABOUT 64 YEARS OLD, SENT TO THE LEFT
JAKAB MARGHIT ABOUT 34 YEARS OLD, NOT SURVIVED

JAKOBI IMRE ABOUT 41 YEARS OLD, NOT SURVIVED
JAKOBI IMRE'S WIFE ABOUT 35 YEARS OLD, NOT SURVIVED

JAKAB TWO BROTHERS ??? YEARS OLD, NOT SURVIVED
JAKAB'S WIVES WITH SIX YOUNG CHILDREN, SENT TO THE LEFT

JOZSEF ELIAS 56 YEARS OLD, SENT TO THE LEFT
JOZSEF ELIAS'S WIFE 48 YEARS OLD, SENT TO THE LEFT
JOZSEF IMRE 26 YEARS OLD, NOT SURVIVED
JOZSEF MIKI 24 YEARS OLD, SURVIVED

JAJCHENEN'S WIDOW ABOUT 44 YEARS OLD, NOT SURVIVED
JAJCHENEN'S FOUR YOUNG CHILDREN 3-16 YEARS OLD, SENT TO THE LEFT
JAJCHENEN'S TWO SONS ABOUT 18 AND 20 YEARS OLD, SURVIVED

KNAPP ABRIS ABOUT 60 YEARS OLD, SENT TO THE LEFT
KNAPP ABRIS'S WIFE ABOUT 56 YEARS OLD, SENT TO THE LEFT
KNAPP ABRIS'S TWO CHILDREN ??? YEARS OLD, NOT SURVIVED

KRELL IZSAK ABOUT 72 YEARS OLD, SENT TO THE LEFT
KRELL IZSAK'S WIFE ABOUT 68 YEARS OLD, SENT TO THE LEFT
KRELL ERNO ABOUT 36 YEARS OLD, SURVIVED

KRELL MIKLOS ABOUT 38 YEARS OLD, NOT SURVIVED
KRELL MIKLOS'S WIFE ABOUT 35 YEARS OLD, NOT SURVIVED
KRELL MIKLOS'S TWO YOUNG CHILDREN, SENT TO THE LEFT

KRELL LAJOS-LUDOVICO ABOUT 34 YEARS OLD, SURVIVED
KRELL'S WIFE, GOLDFRAB ZINA ABOUT 33 YEARS OLD, SURVIVED

KLERMANN BELA ABOUT 45 YEARS OLD, NOT SURVIVED
KLERMANN BELA'S WIFE ABOUT 43 YEARS OLD, NOT SURVIVED
KLERMANN BELA'S SON ABOUT 20 YEARS OLD, NOT SURVIVED

DR. KELLER SAMU 65 YEARS OLD, SENT TO THE LEFT
KELLER MATILD 60 YEARS OLD, SENT TO THE LEFT
KELLER DIDA 30 YEARS OLD, NOT SURVIVED
KELLER FERI ABOUT 25 YEARS OLD, SURVIVED

KOHN ADOLF ABOUT 55 YEARS OLD, SENT TO THE LEFT
KOHN ADOLF'S WIFE ABOUT 53 YEARS OLD, NOT SURVIVED

KLERMANN LAJOS ABOUT 56 YEARS OLD, SENT TO THE LEFT
KLERMANN LAJOS'S WIFE ABOUT 53 YEARS OLD, SENT TO THE LEFT
KLERMANN LAJOS'S DAUGHTER ABOUT 25 YEARS OLD, NOT SURVIVED
KLERMANN SANYI ABOUT 27 YEARS OLD, SURVIVED

KRETS ALADAR ABOUT 42 YEARS OLD, NOT SURVIVED
KRETS'S WIFE, BROD IBI ABOUT 40 YEARS OLD, NOT SURVIVED
KRETS ALADAR'S TWO YOUNG CHILDREN ??? YEARS OLD, NOT SURVIVED

KLEIN NUTE-OIZER ABOUT 55 YEARS OLD, SENT TO THE LEFT
KLEIN NUTE-OIZER'S WIFE ABOUT 50 YEARS OLD, SENT TO THE LEFT
KLEIN SULEM ABOUT 23 YEARS OLD, SURVIVED
KLEIN DASZI ABOUT 20 YEARS OLD, SURVIVED
KLEIN ESZTI ABOUT 17 YEARS OLD, SURVIVED
KLEIN NUTE-OIZER'S OTHER DAUGHTER 14 YEARS OLD, SENT TO THE LEFT

KLEIN GYULA ABOUT 34 YEARS OLD YEARS OLD, NOT SURVIVED
KLEIN'S WIFE, BROD CLARI ABOUT 28 YEARS OLD, SURVIVED

KOHN BENO ABOUT 65 YEARS OLD, SENT TO THE LEFT
KOHN BENO'S WIFE ABOUT 62 YEARS OLD, SENT TO THE LEFT
KOHN BABI 20 YEARS OLD, SURVIVED
KLEIN LAJOS ABOUT 40 YEARS OLD, NOT SURVIVED
KLEIN LAJOS'S WIFE ABOUT 36 YEARS OLD, NOT SURVIVED
KLEIN LAJOS'S SON ABOUT 10 YEARS OLD, SENT TO THE LEFT

KLEIN SANDOR ABOUT 37 YEARS OLD, NOT SURVIVED
KLEIN SANDOR'S WIFE ABOUT 36 YEARS OLD, NOT SURVIVED
KLEIN SANDOR'S DAUGHTER ABOUT 14 YEARS OLD, SENT TO THE LEFT

KRAUSZ AND FAMILY ** UNKNOWN **

KLEIN JENO ABOUT 40 YEARS OLD, NOT SURVIVED
KLEIN JENO'S WIFE ABOUT 39 YEARS OLD, NOT SURVIVED
KLEIN JENO'S THREE YOUNG CHILDREN ??? YEARS OLD, NOT SURVIVED

KLEIN FAMILY ** UNKNOWN **

KELLER IZSO ABOUT 61 YEARS OLD, SENT TO THE LEFT
KELLER IZSO'S WIFE ABOUT 57 YEARS OLD, SENT TO THE LEFT
KELLER KATO DAUGHTER ABOUT 30 YEARS OLD, NOT SURVIVED
KELLER IZSO'S SON ABOUT 28 YEARS OLD, NOT SURVIVED

KLEIN JOZSEF'S WIDOW 72 YEARS OLD, SENT TO THE LEFT

KATZ ABOUT 57 YEARS OLD, NOT SURVIVED
KATZ'S WIFE ABOUT 55 YEARS OLD, NOT SURVIVED
KATZ'S TWO DAUGHTERS ABOUT 25 AND 28 YEARS OLD, NOT SURVIVED

KELLER MOZSI'S WIDOW ABOUT 63 YEARS OLD, SENT TO THE LEFT
KOHN ADOLF ABOUT 70 YEARS OLD, SENT TO THE LEFT
KOHN ADOLF'S WIFE ABOUT 65 YEARS OLD, SENT TO THE LEFT

KISS SANDOR ABOUT 60 YEARS OLD, SENT TO THE LEFT
KISS SANDOR'S WIFE ABOUT 55 YEARS OLD, SENT TO THE LEFT

KISS BUMI ABOUT 37 YEARS OLD, SURVIVED
KISS'S WIFE, BERGER ABOUT 35 YEARS OLD, NOT SURVIVED
KISS HEDI 14 YEARS OLD, SURVIVED
KISS GABRIELLA ABOUT 9 YEARS OLD, SENT TO THE LEFT

KELLER SAMU ABOUT 72 YEARS OLD, SENT TO THE LEFT
KELLER'S WIFE, WEINERGER WIFE ABOUT 69 YEARS OLD, SENT TO THE LEFT
KELLER FERI ABOUT 27 YEARS OLD, SURVIVED
KELLER DIDA AND HER HUSBAND ??? YEARS OLD, NOT SURVIVED

KORNSTEIN ICU ABOUT 40 YEARS OLD, SENT TO THE LEFT
KORNSTEIN RACHEL ABOUT 38 YEARS OLD, NOT SURVIVED
KORNSTEIN GITA ABOUT 18 YEARS OLD, NOT SURVIVED
KORNSTEIN KALMI ABOUT 17 YEARS OLD, NOT SURVIVED

KRETS JAKAB ABOUT 74 YEARS OLD, SENT TO THE LEFT
KRETS-KELLER ETA ABOUT 68 YEARS OLD, SENT TO THE LEFT
KRETS SANDOR ABOUT 40 YEARS OLD, SURVIVED

KRETS-GOLDGLANZ LILI ABOUT 37 YEARS OLD, SURVIVED
KRETS LILI'S FATHER GOLDGLANZ HENRIK 59 YEARS OLD, NOT SURVIVED
KRETS LILI'S MOTHER GOLDGLANZ ETA 57 YEARS OLD, NOT SURVIVED
KRETS LILI'S SISTER GOLDGLANZ NUSI 28 YEARS OLD, NOT SURVIVED
KRETS MATYU ABOUT 20 YEARS OLD, SURVIVED

KONIG ABOUT 45 YEARS OLD, NOT SURVIVED
KONIG'S WIFE ABOUT 40 YEARS OLD, NOT SURVIVED
KONIG'S ADOPTED DAUGHTER ABOUT 10 YEARS OLD, NOT SURVIVED

LAZAR ALBERT ABOUT 70 YEARS OLD, SENT TO THE LEFT
LAZAR ALBERT'S WIFE ABOUT 64 YEARS OLD, SENT TO THE LEFT
LAZAR MAISHE ABOUT 28 YEARS OLD, NOT SURVIVED
LAZAR ILONKA ABOUT 30 YEARS OLD, NOT SURVIVED

LUSZTIG BELA ABOUT 34 YEARS OLD, NOT SURVIVED
LUSZTIG'S WIFE, ROTH ALIZ ABOUT 30 YEARS OLD, SENT TO THE LEFT
LUSZTIG BELA'S SAJE ABOUT 3 YEARS OLD, SENT TO THE LEFT

LOWBEER ARNOLD'S WIDOW ABOUT 66 YEARS OLD, SENT TO THE LEFT
LOWBEER ELEMER 20 YEARS OLD, NOT SURVIVED

LOWBEER NYUSZI-NATHAN ABOUT 35 YEARS OLD, NOT SURVIVED
LOWBEER NYUSZI'S WIFE ABOUT 32 YEARS OLD, NOT SURVIVED

LOWBEER SAMU ABOUT 38 YEARS OLD, NOT SURVIVED
LOWBEER'S WIFE, ULLMANN ABOUT 36 YEARS OLD NOT SURVIVED
LOWBEER SAMU'S TEENAGE SON, SENT TO THE LEFT

LOWBEER FRIGYES ABOUT 40 YEARS OLD, SENT TO THE LEFT
LOWBEER'S WIFE, MARMOSTEIN IREN ABOUT 36 YRS OLD, SENT TO THE LEFT
LOWBEER FRIGYES'S TWO YOUNG CHILDREN, SENT TO THE LEFT

LOWBEER VILMOS ABOUT 30 YEARS OLD, SURVIVED
LOWBEER'S WIFE, WEISZ GABI ABOUT 27 YEARS OLD, SURVIVED

LOWBEER SANDOR'S WIDOW ABOUT 63 YEARS OLD, SENT TO THE LEFT
LOWBEER ERNO ABOUT 30 YEARS OLD, SURVIVED

LOWY JOZSEF-JOSZEF ABOUT 30 YEARS OLD, NOT SURVIVED
LOWY JOZSEF'S WIFE ABOUT 29 YEARS OLD, NOT SURVIVED
LOWY JOZSEF'S TWO YOUNG CHILDREN, SENT TO THE LEFT

LENGYEL MARTON ABOUT 48 YEARS OLD, NOT SURVIVED
LENGYEL MARTON'S WIFE ABOUT 45 YEARS OLD, NOT SURVIVED
LENGYEL SARI ABOUT 18 YEARS OLD, NOT SURVIVED
LENGYEL MARTON'S SON ABOUT 16 YEARS OLD, NOT SURVIVED

LOWINGER ISTVAN ABOUT 35 YEARS OLD, NOT SURVIVED
LOVINGER'S WIFE, GROSZMAN ERZSI ABOUT 30 YEARS OLD, NOT SURVIVED
LOVINGER'S CHILD ABOUT 2 YEARS OLD, SENT TO THE LEFT

LAX SLOMO-SLAIMI ABOUT 39 YEARS OLD, SURVIVED
LAX'S WIFE, BASCH FANI ABOUT 38 YEARS OLD, SENT TO THE LEFT
LAX SLOMO-SLAIMI'S FIVE SMALL CHILDREN, SENT TO THE LEFT

LAX JOZSEF ABOUT 37 YEARS OLD, SURVIVED
LAX JOZSEF'S WIFE ABOUT 35 YEARS OLD, SENT TO THE LEFT
LAX JOZSEF'S THREE SMALL CHILDREN, SENT TO THE LEFT

LAZAR IGNAC'S WIDOW ABOUT 55 YEARS OLD, SENT TO THE LEFT

LAZAR MORIC ABOUT 25 YEARS OLD, NOT SURVIVED

LICHTMAN IGNAC ABOUT 50 YEARS OLD, SENT TO THE LEFT
LICHTMAN'S WIFE, MARTON AMALIA ABOUT 48 YEARS OLD, SENT TO THE LEFT
LICHTMAN BELA ABOUT 26 YEARS OLD, SURVIVED
LICHTMAN JENO ABOUT 24 YEARS OLD, SURVIVED

LEGMANN ADOLF'S WIDOW GIZELLA ABOUT 61 YEARS OLD, SENT TO THE LEFT

LEGMANN ERNO ABOUT 36 YEARS OLD, SURVIVED
LEGMANN ERNO'S TWO SMALL CHILDREN, SENT TO THE LEFT

LEGMANN LAJCSI ABOUT 30 YEARS OLD, SURVIVED
LEGMANN ZALMI 22 YEARS OLD, SURVIVED
LEGMANN TWO OTHER BROTHERS ??? YEARS OLD, NOT SURVIVED

LAUFER SIMON'S WIDOW ABOUT 69 YEARS OLD, SENT TO THE LEFT
LAUFER SIMON'S FOUR MARRIED SONS, ABOUT AGES BETWEEN 25-36 YEARS OLD,
AND THEIR SPOUSES AND CHILDREN, NOT SURVIVED

LEDERER'S WIDOW ABOUT 59 YEARS OLD, SENT TO THE LEFT

LAZAR BELA ABOUT 38 YEARS OLD, SURVIVED
LAZAR BELA'S WIFE ABOUT 35 YEARS OLD & ONE CHILD, NOT SURVIVED

LAZAR GYULA ABOUT 40 YEARS OLD, SURVIVED
LAZAR GYULA'S WIFE ABOUT 39 YEARS OLD, NOT SURVIVED
LAZAR GYULA'S TWO SMALL CHILDREN ??? YEARS OLD, SENT TO THE LEFT

LINDENFELD ABOUT 75 YEARS OLD, SENT TO THE LEFT
LINDENFELD'S WIFE ABOUT 73 YEARS OLD, SENT TO THE LEFT

LAZAROVITS CHEZKEL ABOUT 75 YEARS OLD, SENT TO THE LEFT
LAZAROVITS CHEZKEL'S WIFE ABOUT 70 YEARS OLD, SENT TO THE LEFT

LAMPEL'S WIDOW ABOUT 61 YEARS OLD, SENT TO THE LEFT
LAMPEL MANCI ABOUT 30 YEARS OLD, SURVIVED
LAMPEL JOZSI ABOUT 35 YEARS OLD, NOT SURVIVED

DR. LANG WIDOW ELZA ABOUT 52 YEARS OLD, SENT TO THE LEFT
LANG ELZA'S SON, ROSENBERG BANDI ABOUT 26 YEARS OLD, NOT SURVIVED
LANG ELZA'S 2nd HUSBAND ROSENBERG 58 YRS OLD, SENT TO THE LEFT

MANDEL HANOCH ABOUT 75 YEARS OLD, SENT TO THE LEFT
MANDEL HANOCH'S WIFE ABOUT 70 YEARS OLD, SENT TO THE LEFT
MANDEL HANOCH'S THREE CHILDREN ABOUT 34-40 YEARS OLD, NOT SURVIVED
MANDEL HANOCH'S SON ABOUT 28 YEARS OLD, SURVIVED

MOZES LAZAR ABOUT 50 YEARS OLD, NOT SURVIVED
MOZES LAZAR'S WIFE ABOUT 48 YEARS OLD, NOT SURVIVED
MOZES LAZAR'S SON 25 YEARS OLD, NOT SURVIVED
MOZES NELI ABOUT 17 YEARS OLD, SURVIVED
MOZES ROZSI ABOUT 21 YEARS OLD, SURVIVED

MOSKOVITS NACHAN 53 YEARS OLD, SENT TO THE LEFT
MOSKOVITS MAJSI 32 YEARS OLD, NOT SURVIVED
MOSKOVITS JASZI 28 YEARS OLD, NOT SURVIVED
MOSKOVITS MARTON 25 YEARS OLD, NOT SURVIVED
MOSKOVITS JOLIKA 24 YEARS OLD, NOT SURVIVED
MOSKOVITS ROZSI-RACHEL 22, YEARS OLD, NOT SURVIVED
MOSKOVITS ETA 22 YEARS OLD, YEARS OLD, SURVIVED

MARMOSTEIN HERMAN 65 YEARS OLD, SENT TO THE LEFT
MARMOSTEIN SAROLTA 60 YEARS OLD, SENT TO THE LEFT
MARMOSTEIN IMRE ABOUT 28 YEARS OLD, SURVIVED

MARMOSTEIN MIKLOS-MOSHE ABOUT 33 YEARS OLD, SURVIVED
MARMOSTEIN IREN 31 YEARS OLD, NOT SURVIVED
MARMOSTEIN MATILD 8 YEARS OLD, SENT TO THE LEFT
MARMOSTEIN DEZSO 6 YEARS OLD, SENT TO THE LEFT

MATYAS MATYAS ABOUT 44 YEARS OLD, NOT SURVIVED
MATYAS'S WIFE ABOUT 42 YEARS OLD, NOT SURVIVED
MATYAS'S DAUGHTER ABOUT 20 YEARS OLD, ON THE JOURNEY TO AUSCHWITZ, WAS SENT TO BRING WATER INTO THE CATTLE CAR AND A GUARD SHOT HER
MATYAS PESZI 18 YEARS OLD, SURVIVED
MATYAS SON ABOUT 16 YEARS OLD, NOT SURVIVED
MATYAS SON ABOUT 20 YEARS OLD, SURVIVED

MOZES EIZIK ABOUT 55 YEARS OLD, SENT TO THE LEFT
MOZES EIZIK'S WIFE ABOUT 51 YEARS OLD, WAS SENT TO THE LEFT
MOZES SURI ABOUT 20 YEARS OLD, NOT SURVIVED
MOZES BOSKE ABOUT 25 YEARS OLD, NOT SURVIVED
MOZES LIBU ABOUT 23 YEARS OLD, NOT SURVIVED
MOZES LILI ABOUT 20 YEARS OLD, SURVIVED

MARMOSTEIN JUMI ABOUT 59 YEARS OLD, SENT TO THE LEFT
MARMOSTEIN JUMI'S WIFE ABOUT 58 YEARS OLD, SENT TO THE LEFT
MARMOSTEIN BOSKE ABOUT 33 YEARS OLD, HER HUSBAND ABOUT 36 AND ONE CHILD, NOT SURVIVED
MARMOSTEIN LAICSU ABOUT 22 YEARS OLD, SURVIVED

MOZES DAVID ABOUT 76 YEARS OLD, SENT TO THE LEFT
MOZES DAVID'S WIFE ABOUT 65 YEARS OLD, SENT TO THE LEFT
MOZES DAVID'S TWO SONS ALADAR-ALI AND PALI, NOT SURVIVED
MOZES LILI ABOUT 30 YEARS OLD, SURVIVED
MOZES WILMOS ABOUT 26 YEARS OLD, SURVIVED

MITTELMANN'S WIDOW SARI ABOUT 38 YEARS OLD, NOT SURVIVED
MITTELMANN CLARI 15 YEARS OLD, NOT SURVIVED
MITTELMANN SARI'S SISTER, BERTHA ABOUT 40 YRS OLD, SENT TO THE LEFT

MITTELMANN LAICSI ABOUT 28 YEARS OLD, WORKED IN SIMLEUL, SURVIVED
MITTELMANN ABOUT 60 YEARS OLD, SENT TO THE LEFT
MITTELMANN'S WIFE ABOUT 55 YEARS OLD, SENT TO THE LEFT
MITTELMANN DEZSO ABOUT 28 YEARS OLD, SURVIVED
MITTELMANN GIZI ABOUT 30 YEARS OLD, SURVIVED

MULLER MENDEL ABOUT 40 YEARS OLD, SURVIVED
MULLER GIZELLA 39 YEARS OLD, NOT SURVIVED
MULLER CHAIA 16 YEARS OLD, NOT SURVIVED
MULLER URI 10 YEARS OLD, SENT TO THE LEFT
MULLER HELEN 15 YEARS OLD, SURVIVED

MILITZER LAJOS ABOUT 71 YEARS OLD, SENT TO THE LEFT
MILITZER LAJOS'S WIFE ABOUT 66 YEARS OLD, SENT TO THE LEFT
MILITZER MARICZA ABOUT 28 YEARS OLD, NOT SURVIVED

MILITZER DAVID ABOUT 36 YEARS OLD, NOT SURVIVED
MILITZER DAVID'S WIFE ABOUT 34 YEARS OLD, NOT SURVIVED

MILITZER FERENC ABOUT 40 YEARS OLD, SURVIVED
MILITZER FERENC'S WIFE ABOUT 36 YEARS OLD, NOT SURVIVED

DR. MILITZER JOZSEF ABOUT 38 YEARS OLD, NOT SURVIVED
DR. MILITZER JOZSEF'S WIFE ABOUT 36 YEARS OLD, NOT SURVIVED
MILITZER KATI ABOUT 18 YEARS OLD, NOT SURVIVED
MILITZER PALI ABOUT 23 YEARS OLD, SURVIVED

MARKOVITS SANDOR-SAJE ABOUT 65 YEARS OLD, SENT TO THE LEFT
MARKOVITS ESZTER ABOUT 60 YEARS OLD YEARS OLD, SENT TO THE LEFT
MARKOVITS KRENDI 15 YEARS OLD, NOT SURVIVED
MARKOVITS BERI 13 YEARS OLD, SENT TO THE LEFT
MARKOVITS AJDUKA 10 YEARS OLD SENT TO THE LEFT
MARKOVITS LILI ??? YEARS OLD, SENT TO THE LEFT
MARKOVITS LILI'S FOUR SMALL CHILDREN, SENT TO THE LEFT
MARKOVITS LILI'S HUSBAND ??? YEARS OLD, NOT SURVIVED
MARKOVITS GAD-GYULA ABOUT 36 YEARS OLD, SURVIVED
MARKOVITS ASHER-ZELIG ABOUT 33 YEARS OLD, SURVIVED
MARKOVITS JICCHAK-LICSU ABOUT 30 YEARS OLD, SURVIVED
MARKOVITS DAVID ABOUT 28 YEARS OLD, SURVIVED
MARKOVITS MIRA-MANCI ABOUT 25 YEARS OLD, SURVIVED
MARKOVITS RACHEL-RUKI 22 YEARS OLD, SURVIVED
MARKOVITS CIPORA-BABI ADOPTED BY THE KOHN FAMILY, SURVIVED
MARKOVITS IBOLYA-FRUMI ABOUT 18 YEARS OLD, SURVIVED

MARTON LASZLO ABOUT 35 YEARS OLD, SURVIVED
MARTON LASZLO'S WIFE ABOUT 33 YEARS OLD, NOT SURVIVED
MARTON LASZLO'S CHILDREN 12 AND 14 YEARS OLD, SENT TO THE LEFT

MOSKOVITS SZANE ABOUT 62 YEARS OLD, SENT TO THE LEFT
MOSKOVITS SZANE'S WIFE ABOUT 58 YEARS OLD, SENT TO THE LEFT
MOSKOVITS TOBI ABOUT 22 YEARS OLD, NOT SURVIVED
MOSKOVITS SRULI ABOUT 19 YEARS OLD, NOT SURVIVED
MOSKOVITS ETUKA ABOUT 17 YEARS OLD, NOT SURVIVED
MOSKOVITS BERI ABOUT 15 YEARS OLD, SENT TO THE LEFT
MOSKOVITS ITU ABOUT 10 YEARS OLD, SENT TO THE LEFT
MOSKOVITS PERI ABOUT 8 YEARS OLD, SENT TO THE LEFT
MOSKOVITS HELEN 26 HER HUSBAND 30 AND ONE CHILD SURVIVED IN ROMANIA

MOZES JECHIEL ABOUT 50 YEARS OLD, NOT SURVIVED
MOZES JECHIEL'S WIFE ABOUT 48 YEARS OLD, NOT SURVIVED
MOZES JECHIEL'S THREE YOUNG CHILDREN ??? YEARS OLD, NOT SURVIVED

MENASE (ASSISTANT RABBI) ABOUT 73 YEARS OLD, SENT TO THE LEFT
MENASE'S WIFE ABOUT 70 YEARS OLD, SENT TO THE LEFT

MOZES' WIDOW ABOUT 68 YEARS OLD, SENT TO THE LEFT
MOZES SZURI ABOUT 24 YEARS OLD, NOT SURVIVED
MOZES DINU ABOUT 18 YEARS OLD, NOT SURVIVED
MOZES' ONLY SON ABOUT 25 YEARS OLD, NOT SURVIVED

MARMOSTEIN SAMUEL-SMELKE ABOUT 65 YEARS OLD, SENT TO THE LEFT
MARMOSTEIN-FISCHER LOTI ABOUT 58 YEARS OLD, SENT TO THE LEFT
MARMOSTEIN'S STEPSON FISCHER LACI, SURVIVED

DR. MARKOVITS JAKAB ABOUT 54 YEARS OLD, NOT SURVIVED
DR. MARKOVITS' WIFE ABOUT 50 YEARS OLD, NOT SURVIVED

MOZES HERMAN ABOUT 50 YEARS OLD, SENT TO THE LEFT
MOZES HERMAN'S WIFE ABOUT 48 YEARS OLD, SENT TO THE LEFT
MOZES MANCI ABOUT 25, HER HUSBAND ABOUT 29 YEARS OLD, NOT SURVIVED
MOZES' SON, MAJU ABOUT 20 YEARS OLD, NOT SURVIVED

MEZEI SANDOR ABOUT 45 YEARS OLD, NOT SURVIVED
MEZEI SANDOR'S WIFE ABOUT 42 YEARS OLD, NOT SURVIVED
MEZEI FERI ABOUT 23 YEARS OLD, NOT SURVIVED
MEZEI NELI ABOUT 19 YEARS OLD, NOT SURVIVED

MARGULIESZ FAMILY ** UNKNOWN **

MOSKOVITS JAKAB ABOUT 65 YEARS OLD, SENT TO THE LEFT
MOSKOVITS BOSKE ABOUT 50 YEARS OLD, SENT TO THE LEFT
MOSKOVITS RUCHI ABOUT 10 YEARS OLD, SENT TO THE LEFT
MOSKOVITS BAILI ABOUT 8 YEARS OLD, SENT TO THE LEFT
MOSKOVITS JOSZI ABOUT 5 YEARS OLD, SENT TO THE LEFT

NEUMANN'S WIDOW ABOUT 58 YEARS OLD, SENT TO THE LEFT
NEUMANN PITYU ABOUT 30 YEARS OLD, NOT SURVIVED
NEUMANN LILI ABOUT 35 YEARS OLD, SURVIVED

NASCH FERENC ABOUT 60 YEARS OLD, SENT TO THE LEFT
NASCH FERENC'S WIFE ABOUT 55 YEARS OLD, SENT TO THE LEFT
NASCH HERSHI ABOUT 26 YEARS OLD, NOT SURVIVED
NASCH REZSO 30 YEARS OLD, SURVIVED
NASCH ELIZ 21 YEARS OLD, SURVIVED
NASCH ESZTER ABOUT 20 YEARS OLD, SURVIVED
NASCH MANYI, HER HUSBAND AND CHILDREN, SURVIVED (IN ROMANIA)

NUSSBAUM ARMIN ABOUT 51 YEARS OLD, NOT SURVIVED
NUSSBAUM ARMIN'S WIFE ABOUT 48 YEARS OLD, NOT SURVIVED

NUSSBAUM EVA 18 YEARS OLD EMOTIONALLY DEPRESSED, SURVIVED
NUSSBAUM ARMIN'S SON ABOUT 15 YEARS OLD, SENT TO THE LEFT
NUSSBAUM SAMU ABOUT 40 YEARS OLD, NOT SURVIVED
NUSSBAUM SAMU'S WIFE ABOUT 38 YEARS OLD, NOT SURVIVED
NUSSBAUM MITZI ABOUT 23, HER HUSBAND AND A BABY, NOT SURVIVED
NUSSBAUM JANCSI ABOUT 24 YEARS OLD, RETURNED MENTALLY DISTURBED
AND IN A FEW MONTHS COMMITTED SUICIDE

ORGEL NATHAN ABOUT 70 YEARS OLD, SENT TO THE LEFT
ORGEL NATHAN'S WIFE ABOUT 68 YEARS OLD, SENT TO THE LEFT
ORGEL JOZSEF ABOUT 46 YEARS OLD, NOT SURVIVED
ORGEL JOZSEF'S WIFE ETHEL ABOUT 44 YEARS OLD, NOT SURVIVED
ORGEL MIRIAM ABOUT 20 YEARS OLD, NOT SURVIVED
ORGEL SIMCHA ABOUT 22 YEARS OLD, SURVIVED
ORGEL ITU ABOUT 19 YEARS OLD, SURVIVED
ORGEL BERI ABOUT 17 YEARS OLD, SURVIVED

ORGEL MORDECHAJ ABOUT 44 YEARS OLD, SURVIVED
ORGEL MORDECHAJ'S WIFE ABOUT 42 YRS OLD, NOT SURVIVED
ORGEL SRULI ABOUT 16 YEARS OLD, SURVIVED
ORGEL SIDI ABOUT 20 YEARS OLD, SURVIVED
ORGEL TOSHI ABOUT 18 YEARS OLD, SURVIVED

ORGEL BUMI ABOUT 38 YEARS OLD, NOT SURVIVED
ORGEL BUMI'S WIFE ABOUT 36 YEARS OLD, NOT SURVIVED

PASZTERNAK SAMUEL 68 YEARS OLD, SENT TO THE LEFT
PASZTERNAK SAMUEL'S WIFE 65 YEARS, OLD SENT TO THE LEFT

POLLAK IMRE ABOUT 24 YEARS OLD, SURVIVED
POLLAK-KLEIN MAGDA ABOUT 20 YEARS OLD, NOT SURVIVED

POLLAK SANDOR ABOUT 32 YEARS OLD, NOT SURVIVED
POLLAK SANDOR'S WIFE ABOUT 30 YEARS OLD, NOT SURVIVED

PERLMUTTER NAFTALI'S WIDOW ABOUT 72 YEARS OLD, SENT TO THE LEFT
PERLMUTTER JOSZEF-DAVID ABOUT 28 YEARS OLD, NOT SURVIVED
PERLMUTTER ZVI ABOUT 25 YEARS OLD, NOT SURVIVED
PERLMUTTER SARA-RIVKA ABOUT 30 YEARS OLD, NOT SURVIVED
PERLMUTTER SARA'S HUSBAND AND CHILD ??? YEARS OLD, NOT SURVIVED
PERLMUTTER RACHEL-LEA ABOUT 22 YEARS OLD, NOT SURVIVED
PERLMUTTER MOSHE ABOUT 20 YEARS OLD, SURVIVED

PINCHASZ STULL ABOUT 40 YEARS OLD, NOT SURVIVED
PINCHASZ STULL'S WIFE ABOUT 38 YEARS OLD, NOT SURVIVED
PINCHASZ'S FOUR YOUNG CHILDREN ABOUT 3, 6, 9, AND 12 YEARS OLD, SENT TO THE LEFT

DR. PORJESZ ALADAR ABOUT 50 YEARS OLD, NOT SURVIVED
DR. PORJESZ ALADAR'S MOTHER ABOUT 72 YEARS OLD, SENT TO THE LEFT

POLLAK MATYAS ABOUT 68 YEARS OLD, SENT TO THE LEFT
POLLAK MATYAS' WIFE ABOUT 65 YEARS OLD, SENT TO THE LEFT
POLLAK SARI 18 YEARS OLD SURVIVED **SS** DOCTORS DID EXPERIMENTS
ON HER KNEES; THE OPEN WOUND NEVER HEALED & WITHIN A FEW MONTHS SHE DIED.
POLLAK MIKLOS ABOUT 38 YEARS OLD, SURVIVED
POLLAK-BRIER IREN ABOUT 37 YEARS OLD, SURVIVED

PERLMUTTER HANOCH ABOUT 69 YEARS OLD, SENT TO THE LEFT
PERLMUTTER HANOCH'S WIFE ABOUT 64 YEARS OLD, SENT TO THE LEFT
PERLMUTTER SMILU ABOUT 36 YEARS OLD, NOT SURVIVED ???

PERLMUTTER SMIL-DUVED'S WIDOW ABOUT 45 YEARS OLD, NOT SURVIVED
PERLMUTTER SMIL'S FIVE CHILDREN ??? YEARS OLD, SENT TO THE LEFT

PERLMUTTER'S WIDOW (CHAJA-PINKL) & FOUR CHILDREN, NOT SURVIVED

PREISLER ALADAR ABOUT 58 YEARS OLD, SENT TO THE LEFT
PREISLER ALADAR'S WIFE ABOUT 55 YEARS OLD, SENT TO THE LEFT
PREISLER ALADAR'S CHILD ABOUT 25 YEARS OLD, SURVIVED

ROTH JAKAB ABOUT 55 YEARS OLD, NOT SURVIVED
ROTH JAKAB'S WIFE ABOUT 50 YEARS OLD, NOT SURVIVED
ROTH JAKAB'S DAUGHTER AND SON ??? YEARS OLD, NOT SURVIVED

DR. ROSENBERG ZOLTAN ABOUT 45 YEARS OLD, NOT SURVIVED
DR. ROSENBERG ZOLTAN'S WIFE ABOUT 42 YEARS OLD, NOT SURVIVED

ROSENBERG ELJE ABOUT 58 YEARS OLD, SENT TO THE LEFT
ROSENBERG ELJE'S WIFE ABOUT 55 YEARS OLD, SENT TO THE LEFT
ROSENBERG ELJE'S TWO CHILDREN ??? YEARS OLD, NOT SURVIVED

ROSENBERG MOR-MAJSE AND FAMILY ** UNKNOWN **

ROSENBERG REUVEN AND FAMILY ** UNKNOWN **

ROSENBERG JANKU-JAAKOV ABOUT 35 YEARS OLD, NOT SURVIVED
ROSENBERG JANKU'S WIFE ABOUT 32 YEARS OLD, NOT SURVIVED
ROSENBERG'S 3 DAUGHTERS ABOUT 15, 13 & 10 YRS OLD, SENT TO THE LEFT

ROSENBERG SANDOR ABOUT 41 YEARS OLD, NOT SURVIVED
ROSENBERG SANDOR'S WIFE ABOUT 40 YEARS OLD, NOT SURVIVED
ROSENBERG BIDU ABOUT 19 YEARS OLD, NOT SURVIVED

ROSENBERG SZIMCHE ABOUT ??? YEARS OLD, NOT SURVIVED
ROSENBERG SZIMCHE'S WIFE ??? ABOUT YEARS OLD, NOT SURVIVED

ROSENBERG BELA (DOV-BER) ABOUT 43 YEARS OLD, SURVIVED
ROSENBERG'S WIFE, BLAU NUSI ABOUT 37 YEARS OLD, NOT SURVIVED
R. NUSI'S SISTER, BLAU RAIZI ABOUT 22 YEARS OLD, NOT SURVIVED

REISMANN SAMU ABOUT 48 YEARS OLD, NOT SURVIVED
REISMANN SAMU'S WIFE ABOUT 44 YEARS OLD, NOT SURVIVED
REISMANN SAMU'S DAUGHTER ABOUT 20 YEARS OLD, NOT SURVIVED
REISMANN SAMU'S SON ABOUT 18 YEARS OLD, NOT SURVIVED

ROSENBERG SAMUEL'S WIDOW ABOUT 60 YEARS OLD, SENT TO

THE LEFT
ROTTENSTEIN'S WIDOW ABOUT 73 YEARS OLD, SENT TO THE LEFT

ROSENBERG DEZSO ABOUT 36 YEARS OLD , NOT SURVIVED
ROSENBERG DEZSO'S WIFE ABOUT 35 YEARS OLD, NOT SURVIVED

ROSENBERG HILLEL ABOUT 48 YEARS OLD, NOT SURVIVED
ROSENBERG HILLEL'S WIFE ABOUT 46 YEARS OLD, NOT SURVIVED
ROSENBERG GEZA ABOUT 24 YEARS OLD, NOT SURVIVED
ROSENBERG TERI ABOUT 22 YEARS OLD, NOT SURVIVED

ROTH FERI ABOUT 58 YEARS OLD, SENT TO THE LEFT
ROTH FERI'S WIFE ABOUT 55 YEARS OLD, SENT TO THE LEFT
ROTH FERI'S TWO CHILDREN ??? YEARS OLD, NOT SURVIVED

ROSENZWEIG ABOUT 42 YEARS OLD, NOT SURVIVED
ROSENZWEIG'S WIFE ABOUT 40 YEARS OLD, NOT SURVIVED
ROSENZWEIG EVA 19 YEARS OLD, NOT SURVIVED

ROSENFELD LAJOS ABOUT 64 YEARS OLD, SENT TO THE LEFT
ROSENFELD LAJOS'S WIFE ABOUT 60 YEARS OLD, SENT TO THE LEFT
ROSENFELD BOSKE ABOUT 25 YEARS OLD, NOT SURVIVED
ROSENFELD KITU ABOUT 22 YEARS OLD, SURVIVED

RUSZ ELIAS ABOUT 70 YEARS OLD, SENT TO THE LEFT
RUSZ ELIAS' WIFE ABOUT 68 YEARS OLD, SENT TO THE LEFT
RUSZ ELIAS' SONS ABOUT 34 AND 36 YEARS OLD, NOT SURVIVED
RUSZ ELIAS' DAUGHTER ABOUT 38 AND 30 YEARS OLD, NOT SURVIVED

RUTNER MENDEL ABOUT 30 YEARS OLD, SURVIVED
RUTNER HAIE ABOUT 25 YEARS OLD, SURVIVED
RUTNER MANDEL AND HAIE'S BABY, SENT TO THE LEFT

ROTSCHILD JENO ABOUT 45 YEARS OLD, NOT SURVIVED
ROTSCHILD-ULLMANN HEDI ABOUT 42 YEARS OLD, NOT SURVIVED
ROTSCHILD'S CHILD ABOUT 20 YEARS OLD, NOT SURVIVED

ROTH IZIDOR ABOUT 78 YEARS OLD, SENT TO THE LEFT
ROTH IZIDOR'S WIFE ABOUT 72 YEARS OLD, SENT TO THE LEFT

REICHER ABOUT 46 YEARS OLD, NOT SURVIVED
REICHER'S WIFE ABOUT 45 YEARS OLD, NOT SURVIVED
REICHER'S TWO DAUGHTERS ABOUT 15 AND 22 YEARS OLD, NOT SURVIVED
REICHER CIPRI 18 YEARS OLD, SURVIVED

SALAMON ABOUT 64 YEARS OLD, SENT TO THE LEFT
SALAMON'S WIFE ABOUT 60 YEARS OLD, SENT TO THE LEFT
SALAMON'S FOUR DAUGHTERS ABOUT 26-34 YEARS OLD, NOT SURVIVED

SILBERSTEIN SAMUEL ABOUT 36 YEARS OLD, NOT SURVIVED
SILBERSTEIN'S WIFE, BASCH ROZSI ABOUT 36 YEARS OLD, NOT SURVIVED
SILBERSTEIN SAMUEL'S FOUR YOUNG CHILDREN, SENT TO THE LEFT

SZEP ADOLF ABOUT 53 YEARS OLD, NOT SURVIVED
SZEP ADOLF'S WIFE ABOUT 49 YEARS OLD, NOT SURVIVED
SZEP MATZU ABOUT 23 YEARS OLD, NOT SURVIVED
SZEP ILUS ABOUT 28, HER HUSBAND ABOUT 33 YEARS OLD, NOT SURVIVED
SZEP ILUS'S TWO YOUNG CHILDREN, SENT TO THE LEFT

SCHWARTZ MORITZ AND FAMILY ** UNKNOWN **

SOMOGYI SANDOR ABOUT 65 YEARS OLD, SENT TO THE LEFT
SOMOGYI SANDOR'S WIFE ABOUT 63 YEARS OLD, SENT TO THE LEFT

DR. SOMOGYI FERENC ABOUT 38 YEARS OLD, NOT SURVIVED
DR. SOMOGYI'S WIFE, STEINER ABOUT 36 YEARS OLD AND ONE YOUNG CHILD, NOT SURVIVED

DR. SAMUEL VILMOS ABOUT 50 YEARS OLD, NOT SURVIVED
DR. SAMUEL WILMOS'S WIFE ABOUT 48 YEARS OLD, NOT SURVIVED
SAMUEL JANCSI-PISTI ABOUT 24 YEARS OLD, NOT SURVIVED
SAMUEL SISI ABOUT 26 YEARS OLD, ** UNKNOWN ** ????????
SAMUEL SISI'S HUSBAND ABOUT 31 YEARS OLD, NOT SURVIVED
SAMUEL SISI'S BABY, SENT TO THE LEFT

DR. SPETER HENRIK (BABA) ABOUT 43 YEARS OLD, SURVIVED

STEINER LAJOS ABOUT 60 YEARS OLD, NOT SURVIVED
STEINER LAJOS'S WIFE ABOUT 55 YEARS OLD, NOT SURVIVED
STEINER'S 3 DAUGHTERS ABOUT 24, 27, AND 30 YEARS OLD, NOT SURVIVED
SCHWARTZ'S WIDOW ABOUT 57 YEARS OLD, SENT TO THE LEFT
SCHWARTZ ITCHAK ABOUT 20 YEARS OLD, NOT SURVIVED
SCHWARTZ CHUNE ABOUT 18 YEARS OLD, NOT SURVIVED
SCHWARTZ LIPU ABOUT 22 YEARS OLD, SURVIVED

STEINMETZ CHEZKEL ABOUT 66 YEARS OLD, SENT TO THE LEFT
STEINMETZ CHEZKEL'S WIFE ABOUT 63 YEARS OLD, SENT TO THE LEFT
STEINMETZ'S FOUR CHILDREN, THEIR FAMILIES, NOT SURVIVED

STERNBERG ABOUT 60 YEARS OLD, SENT TO THE LEFT
STEINBERG'S WIFE ABOUT 58 YEARS OLD, SENT TO THE LEFT
STEINBERG'S SON ABOUT 26 YEARS OLD, NOT SURVIVED

STERN LIPOT ABOUT 50 YEARS OLD, SENT TO THE LEFT
STERN LIPOT'S WIFE ABOUT 50 YEARS OLD, SENT TO THE LEFT
STERN LIPOT'S TWO DAUGHTERS ABOUT 20 AND 22 YEARS OLD, NOT SURVIVED
STERN LIPOT'S SONS ABOUT 24 AND 18 YEARS OLD, SURVIVED

SCHACHTER IZIDOR ABOUT 55 YEARS OLD, SENT TO THE LEFT
SCHACHTER IZIDOR'S WIFE ABOUT 50 YEARS OLD, SENT TO THE LEFT
SCHACHTER AJDI ABOUT 35 YRS OLD, HER HUSBAND ABOUT 37 YEARS OLD, AND A YOUNG CHILD, NOT SURVIVED

SCHACHTER NUSZI (AVRUM-NUSZEN) ABOUT 30 YEARS OLD, NOT SURVIVED
SCHACHTER NUSZI'S WIFE ABOUT 28 AND ONE CHILD, NOT SURVIVED
SZALAVETZ MENDEL ABOUT 50 YEARS OLD, NOT SURVIVED
SZALAVETZ MENDEL'S WIFE ABOUT 48 YEARS OLD, NOT SURVIVED
SZALAVETZ SURI ABOUT 24 YEARS OLD, NOT SURVIVED

SURI'S HUSBAND POLLAK FERI ABOUT 28 YEARS OLD, NOT SURVIVED
SURI'S AND POLLAK FERI'S BABY, SENT TO THE LEFT
SZALAVETZ HESZKU ABOUT 12 YEARS OLD, SENT TO THE LEFT
SZALAVETZ'S THREE SONS ABOUT 18, 20, AND 22 YEARS OLD, SURVIVED

STEINER'S WIDOW ABOUT 61 YEARS OLD, SENT TO THE LEFT

SCHWARTZ ABRAHAM AND FAMILY ** UNKNOWN **

STERN MOSHE ABOUT 41 YEARS OLD, SURVIVED
STERN'S WIFE, HEIMLICH HERMINA ABOUT 39 YEARS OLD, SENT TO THE LEFT
STERN JOSZEF-AVRAM 16 YEARS, NOT SURVIVED
STERN BABA-RACHEL 14 YEARS OLD, SENT TO THE LEFT
STERN JANKI-JAKOV 9 YEARS OLD, SENT TO THE LEFT
STERN MOSHE'S MOTHER, FEIGE BERKOVITS 73 YRS OLD, SENT TO THE LEFT
STERN MOSHE'S GRANDFATHER BERKOVITS LORINC, SENT TO THE LEFT
STERN MOSHE'S GRANDMOTHER BERKOVITS-POLLAK DVORA, SENT TO THE LEFT

SCHON IGNAC ABOUT 42 YEARS OLD, SURVIVED
SCHON IGNAC'S WIFE ABOUT 40 YEARS OLD, NOT SURVIVED
SCHON IGNAC'S SON ABOUT 18 YEARS OLD, NOT SURVIVED

SAMUEL LAZAR 68 YEARS OLD, SENT TO THE LEFT
SAMUEL NATI 65 YEARS OLD, SENT TO THE LEFT
SAMUEL IREN MARRIED (LEGMANN) 38 YEARS OLD, NOT SURVIVED
SAMUEL IREN'S SON, LEGMANN LACI 16 YEARS OLD, NOT SURVIVED
SAMUEL IREN'S DAUGHTER, LEGMANN LIA 8 YEARS OLD, SENT TO THE LEFT

SAMUEL ERNO ABOUT 38 YEARS OLD, SURVIVED
SAMUEL ERNO'S WIFE STEFANIA 33 YEARS OLD, NOT SURVIVED
SAMUEL ERNO'S DAUGHTER ILA 6 YEARS OLD, SENT TO THE LEFT

SAMUEL ELEK ABOUT 55 YEARS OLD, SENT TO THE LEFT
SAMUEL ELEK'S MOTHER ABOUT 77 YEARS OLD, SENT TO THE LEFT

STERN LUIZA ABOUT 48 YEARS OLD, SENT TO THE LEFT
STERN L. HUSBAND FEUERWERKER HERMAN 50 YEARS OLD, SENT TO THE LEFT
STERN L. SON FEUERWERKER AVRAM-JOSZEF 15 YEARS OLD, THE LEFT
STERN L. SON FEUERWERKER J. JAKOV 13 YEARS OLD, SENT TO THE LEFT
STERN L. SON FEUERWERKER FISCHEL ABOUT 20 YEARS OLD, SURVIVED
SAMUEL LUIZA AND FAMILY ** UNKNOWN **

SAMUEL JOZSEF ABOUT 39 YEARS OLD, NOT SURVIVED
SAMUEL JOZSEF'S WIFE ABOUT 36 YEARS OLD, NOT SURVIVED
SAMUEL JOZSEF'S SON ABOUT 16 YEARS OLD, NOT SURVIVED

SCHVALB ABOUT 40 YEARS OLD, NOT SURVIVED
SCHVALB'S WIFE ABOUT 38 YEARS OLD, SON AND DAUGHTER, NOT SURVIVED
SILBERSTEIN SAMUEL ABOUT 38 YEARS OLD, NOT SURVIVED
SILBERSTEIN-BASCH LILI ABOUT 36 YEARS OLD, NOT SURVIVED
SILBERSTEIN'S THREE YOUNG CHILDREN ??? YEARS OLD, SENT TO THE LEFT

SALAMON ABOUT 59 YEARS OLD, SENT TO THE LEFT
SALAMON'S WIFE ABOUT 57 YEARS OLD, SENT TO THE LEFT

SAMUEL SANDOR ABOUT 50 YEARS OLD, NOT SURVIVED
SAMUEL SANDOR'S WIFE ABOUT 48 YEARS OLD, NOT SURVIVED
SAMUEL SZEREN ABOUT 23 YEARS OLD, SURVIVED

SZILAGYI DEZSO ABOUT 52 YEARS OLD, SENT TO THE LEFT
SZILAGYI'S WIFE IDA ABOUT 50 YEARS OLD, SENT TO THE LEFT
SZILAGYI IREN ABOUT 28 YEARS OLD, SURVIVED
SZILAGYI ERZSI ABOUT 26 YEARS OLD, SURVIVED

STERN ADOLF'S ABOUT 66 YEARS OLD, NOT SURVIVED
STERN BANDI ABOUT 28 YEARS OLD, NOT SURVIVED
STERN PALI ABOUT 24 YEARS OLD, NOT SURVIVED
STERN ADOLF'S TWO DAUGHTERS NOT SURVIVED

STEINER MARTON ABOUT 40 YEARS OLD, SURVIVED
STEINER'S WIFE, HARSTEIN BELLA ABOUT 38 YEARS OLD, SENT TO THE LEFT
STEINER KATO 15 YEARS OLD, SENT TO THE LEFT
STEINER PISTI 12 YEARS OLD, SENT TO THE LEFT

SCHREIBER LAJOS (JICHAK-JUDA) ABOUT 52 YEARS OLD, NOT SURVIVED
SCHREIBER-CSENGERI ARANKA ABOUT 50 YEARS OLD, NOT SURVIVED
SCHREIBER ERVIN-SHMUEL 22 YEARS OLD, NOT SURVIVED
SCHREIBER PAL-BIMBI 20 YEARS OLD, NOT SURVIVED
SCHREIBER PERETZ 18 YEARS OLD, SURVIVED

SCHWARTZ IGNATC'S WIDOW ABOUT 58 YEARS OLD, SENT TO THE LEFT

SILBERSTEIN MORIC ABOUT 41 YEARS OLD, NOT SURVIVED
SILBERSTEIN'S WIFE, KRELL LUCY ABOUT 38 YEARS OLD, NOT SURVIVED
SILBERSTEIN ANDRIS 11 YEARS OLD, SENT TO THE LEFT
SILBERSTEIN KAROLY ABOUT 21 YEARS OLD, SURVIVED

DR. SZEKELY SANDOR ABOUT 50 YEARS OLD, NOT SURVIVED
DR. SZEKELY SANDOR'S WIFE ABOUT 48 YEARS OLD, NOT SURVIVED
SZEKELY MARTHA ABOUT 18 YEARS OLD, NOT SURVIVED
SZEKELY PISTA ABOUT 15 YEARS OLD, NOT SURVIVED

SALAMON'S WIDOW 56 YEARS OLD, SENT TO THE LEFT
SALAMON'S TWO DAUGHTERS ABOUT 26 AND 22 YRS OLD, NOT SURVIVED

SAKTER'S WIDOW AND FOUR CHILDREN, NOT SURVIVED ** UNKNOWN **

SIJE PINCHESZ WEISZ ABOUT 55 YEARS OLD, NOT SURVIVED
SIJE PINCHESZ'S WIFE ABOUT 50 YEARS OLD, NOT SURVIVED
SIJE PINCHESZ'S FIVE CHILDREN ??? YEARS OLD, NOT SURVIVED

SCHWARTZ ETELKA AND FAMILY ** UNKNOWN **
SALAMON'S WIDOW ABOUT 53 YEARS OLD, NOT SURVIVED
SALAMON RENE ABOUT 30 YEARS OLD, NOT SURVIVED
SALAMON LAJOS ABOUT 30 YEARS OLD, NOT SURVIVED

ULLMANN IGNAC ABOUT 62 YEARS OLD, SENT TO THE LEFT
ULLMANN IGNAC'S WIFE ABOUT 58 YEARS OLD, SENT TO THE LEFT
ULLMANN NANDOR ABOUT 38 YEARS OLD, NOT SURVIVED
ULLMANN GYULA ABOUT 36 YEARS OLD, SURVIVED
ULLMANN IGNAC'S DAUGHTERS ABOUT 28, 33 YEARS OLD, NOT SURVIVED

UNGAR MENDEL ABOUT 60 YEARS OLD, SENT TO THE LEFT
UNGAR MENDEL'S WIFE ABOUT 57 YEARS OLD, SENT TO THE LEFT
UNGAR MENDEL'S TWO CHILDREN ??? YEARS OLD, NOT SURVIVED

UNGAR JOZSEF AND FAMILY ** UNKNOWN **

UNGAR MORIC ABOUT 56 YEARS OLD, NOT SURVIVED
UNGAR MORIC'S WIFE ABOUT 48 YEARS OLD NOT SURVIVED
UNGAR'S SON AND DAUGHTER ABOUT YEARS OLD ???, NOT SURVIVED

DR. UNGAR IGNAC ABOUT 60 YEARS OLD, SENT TO THE LEFT
DR. UNGAR'S WIFE ABOUT 57 YEARS OLD, SENT TO THE LEFT
DR. UNGAR'S 3 MARRIED CHILDREN AND THEIR FAMILIES, NOT SURVIVED

WEISZ SALAMON ABOUT 70 YEARS OLD, SENT TO THE LEFT
WEISZ'S WIFE, SZEREN ABOUT 68 YEARS OLD, SENT TO THE LEFT

WEISZ MIKLOS ABOUT 30 YEARS OLD, SURVIVED
WEISZ MIKLOS'S WIFE, ROZSI ABOUT 28 YEARS OLD, NOT SURVIVED

WEISZ RUDOLF ABOUT 28 YEARS OLD, SURVIVED
WEISZ RUDOLF'S WIFE, KLARA ABOUT 25 YEARS OLD, NOT SURVIVED

WEISZ NAFTALI-HERS AND FAMILY ** UNKNOWN **

WEISZ JOZSEF-JERUCHEM ABOUT 56 YEARS OLD, SENT TO THE LEFT
WEISZ JOZSEF'S WIFE ABOUT 50 YEARS OLD, SENT TO THE LEFT
WEISZ JOZSEF'S TWO CHILDREN ??? YEARS OLD, NOT SURVIVED

DR. WEISZ SAMU ABOUT 55 YEARS OLD, NOT SURVIVED
DR. WEISZ SAMU'S WIFE ABOUT 50 YEARS OLD, NOT SURVIVED
WEISZ GABRIELLA ABOUT 26 YEARS OLD, NOT SURVIVED
WEISZ SARI ABOUT 24 YEARS OLD, NOT SURVIVED
WEISZ JOSKA ABOUT 22 YEARS OLD, NOT SURVIVED
WEISZ SANDOR ABOUT 28 YEARS OLD, NOT SURVIVED

VADASZ ETELKA ABOUT 46 YEARS OLD, NOT SURVIVED
VADASZ ETELKA'S HUSBAND ABOUT 47 YEARS OLD, NOT SURVIVED
VADASZ PUTYU 19 YEARS OLD, NOT SURVIVED
VADASZ SARI 17 YEARS OLD, NOT SURVIVED
VADASZ OCSI 15 YEARS OLD, NOT SURVIVED
DR. WEINBERGER GYULA ABOUT 48 YEARS OLD, NOT SURVIVED
WEINBERGER GYULA'S WIFE ABOUT 44 YEARS OLD, NOT SURVIVED
WEINBERGER PALI 18 YEARS OLD, SURVIVED
WEINBERGER PALMA ABOUT 20 YEARS OLD, SURVIVED

WEINBERGER'S WIDOW (CILIMAMA) ABOUT 79 YEARS OLD, SENT TO THE LEFT
WEINBERGER ROZSI ABOUT 45 YEARS OLD, NOT SURVIVED

WEISZ EFRAIM'S WIDOW ABOUT 58 YEARS OLD, SENT TO THE LEFT
WEISZ RICKI ABOUT 20 YEARS OLD, NOT SURVIVED
WEISZ EFRAIM'S DAUGHTER ABOUT 25 YEARS OLD, NOT SURVIVED

WEISZ EFRAIM'S SON ABOUT 29 YEARS OLD, NOT SURVIVED
WEISZ MOR ABOUT 56 YEARS OLD, NOT SURVIVED
WEISZ MOR'S WIFE ABOUT 49 YEARS OLD, NOT SURVIVED
WEISZ MOR'S SON ABOUT 34 YEARS OLD, NOT SURVIVED
WEISZ AGI ABOUT 20 YEARS OLD, NOT SURVIVED
WEISZ ERZSI ABOUT 22 YEARS OLD, SURVIVED

WIEDER'S WIDOW ABOUT 69 YEARS OLD, SENT TO THE LEFT

WEISZ DORI ABOUT 50 YEARS OLD, NOT SURVIVED
WEISZ DORI'S WIFE ABOUT 46 YEARS OLD, NOT SURVIVED
WEISZ IBI 19 YEARS OLD GOT A COLD AND KILLED IN AUSCHWITZ
WEISZ SANYI ABOUT 22 YEARS OLD SURVIVED, BUT WAS SHOT AT THE BORDER
WEISZ DORI'S OTHER SON ABOUT 15 YEARS OLD, SENT TO THE LEFT

WIEDER SIMON ABOUT 48 YEARS OLD, SENT TO THE LEFT
WIEDER SIMON'S WIFE ABOUT 42 YEARS OLD, SENT TO THE LEFT
WIEDER CHAJIM 7 YEARS OLD, SENT TO THE LEFT
WIEDER PASTS-JUDITH 17 YEARS OLD, SURVIVED
WIEDER MINCZI ABOUT 22 YEARS OLD, SURVIVED
WIEDER ZOLTAN ABOUT 20 YEARS OLD, SURVIVED

WIEDER MENDL-BAR ABOUT 38 YEARS OLD, NOT SURVIVED
WIEDER MENDL'S WIFE ABOUT 37 YEARS OLD SURVIVED
WIEDER MIRJAM ABOUT 16 YEARS OLD, NOT SURVIVED
WIEDER VALVI ABOUT 13 YEARS OLD, SENT TO THE LEFT
WIEDER JUDA ABOUT 10 YEARS OLD, SENT TO THE LEFT

WEISZ SAMUEL 59 YEARS OLD, SENT TO THE LEFT
WEISZ'S WIFE EHRENFELD GIZELLA 56 YEARS OLD, SENT TO THE LEFT
WEISZ ALBIN 23 YEARS OLD, NOT SURVIVED
WEISZ EUGEN 21 YEARS OLD, NOT SURVIVED
WEISZ MAURICIU 19 YEARS OLD, NOT SURVIVED
WEISZ ARTHUR 14 YEARS OLD, SENT TO THE LEFT
WEISZ ERNEST 12 YEARS OLD, SENT TO THE LEFT
WEISZ VALERIA 22 YEARS OLD, NOT SURVIVED
WEISZ OLGA 20 YEARS OLD, NOT SURVIVED
WEISZ LIVIA 15 YEARS OLD, SENT TO THE LEFT
WEISZ ERNA 10 YEARS OLD, SENT TO THE LEFT
WEISZ EDUARD-CHAJIM ABOUT 17 YEARS OLD WITH TUBERCULOSIS, SURVIVED

WEBERMANN'S WIDOW, ROZA 62 YEARS OLD, SENT TO THE LEFT
WEBERMANN ZVI ABOUT 32 YEARS OLD, SURVIVED
WEBERMANN ROZA'S SON, SCHWARTZ DEZSO 38 YEARS OLD, NOT SURVIVED
WEBERMANN ROZA'S SON, SCHWARTZ ANDOR ABOUT 34 YEARS OLD, SURVIVED

WELLER ZISZE ABOUT 65 YEARS OLD, SENT TO THE LEFT

WELLER ZISZE'S WIFE ABOUT 60 YEARS OLD, SENT TO THE LEFT
WELLER AVRUM ABOUT 40 YEARS OLD, HIS WIFE ABOUT 38 YEARS OLD, THEIR FOUR YOUNG CHILDREN, NOT SURVIVED
WELLER ELIJE ABOUT 20 YEARS OLD SURVIVED

WIEDER ARON-ZVI ABOUT 30 YEARS OLD, NOT SURVIVED
WIEDER'S WIFE ABOUT 35 YEARS OLD AND TWO SON'S, NOT SURVIVED
WEISZ FERENC ABOUT 40 YEARS OLD, NOT SURVIVED
WEISZ FERENC'S WIFE ABOUT 38 YEARS OLD AND TWO TEENAGE DAUGHTERS
ABOUT 14 AND 16 YEARS OLD, NOT SURVIVED

WEISZ ARNOLD ABOUT 60 YEARS OLD, SENT TO THE LEFT
WEISZ ARNOLD'S WIFE ABOUT 58 YEARS OLD, SENT TO THE LEFT
WEISZ JASZI ABOUT 34 YRS OLD, SURVIVED
WEISZ JASZI'S WIFE ABOUT 30 YEARS OLD AND CHILDREN, NOT SURVIVED
WEISZ DAVID ABOUT 32 YRS, HIS WIFE AND CHILDREN, NOT SURVIVED
WEISZ SLAIME ABOUT 28 YEARS OLD AND HIS WIFE, NOT SURVIVED

WEISZ SALAMON ABOUT 75 YEARS OLD, SENT TO THE LEFT
WEISZ SALAMON'S WIFE ABOUT 70 YEARS OLD, SENT TO THE LEFT

WEISZ ELEK'S WIDOW ABOUT 78 YEARS OLD, SENT TO THE LEFT

WEISZ HENRIK (CHAIM ZVI) ABOUT 54 YEARS OLD, SENT TO THE LEFT
WEISZ HENRIK'S WIFE ABOUT 53 YEARS OLD, SENT TO THE LEFT
WEISZ GITU 15 YEARS OLD, SENT TO THE LEFT
WEISZ JENTI ABOUT 23 YEARS OLD, NOT SURVIVED
WEISZ CHAIEM-HERS ABOUT 23 YEARS OLD, SURVIVED
WEISZ SIJU ABOUT 21 YEARS OLD, SURVIVED

WEISZ SAMUEL 46 YEARS OLD, SENT TO THE LEFT
WEISZ BELA 18 YEARS OLD, SURVIVED
WEISZ ELKU 17 YEARS OLD, NOT SURVIVED
WEISZ-LOVI ESTER 72 YEARS OLD, SENT TO THE LEFT

WEISZ JENO ABOUT 38 YEARS OLD, NOT SURVIVED
WEISZ-ENGEL JOLAN ABOUT 36 YEARS OLD, NOT SURVIVED
WEISZ IVAN ABOUT 12 YEARS OLD, SENT TO THE LEFT
WEISZ OCSI ABOUT 10 YEARS OLD, SENT TO THE LEFT

WEISZ ZALMAN-LEIB ABOUT 75 YEARS OLD, SENT TO THE LEFT
WEISZ ZALMAN'S WIFE ABOUT 70 YEARS OLD, SENT TO THE LEFT

WEISZ JOZSEF ABOUT 40 YEARS OLD, NOT SURVIVED
WEISZ'S WIFE, MARMOSTEIN IRENKE ABOUT 38 YEARS OLD, NOT SURVIVED
WEISZ LEZER ABOUT 17 YEARS OLD, NOT SURVIVED
WEISZ DUCI ABOUT 13 YEARS OLD, SENT TO THE LEFT
WEISZ RIFKA ABOUT 10 YEARS OLD, SENT TO THE LEFT
WEISZ JOZSEF'S SON ABOUT 7 YEARS OLD, SENT TO THE LEFT

WEISZ ERNO-EZRA ABOUT 40 YEARS OLD, SURVIVED
WEISZ'S WIFE, CZEIZLER ELLA ABOUT 38 YEARS OLD, NOT SURVIVED
WEISZ ERNO'S SONS ABOUT 16 AND 13 YEARS OLD, NOT SURVIVED
WEISZ ERNO'S DAUGHTERS ABOUT 10 AND 8 YEARS OLD, NOT SURVIVED

DR. WEINBERGER ZOLTAN ABOUT 48 YEARS OLD, NOT SURVIVED
DR. WEINBERGER'S WIFE ABOUT 40 YEARS OLD, NOT SURVIVED
WEINBERGER'S TWO DAUGHTERS ABOUT 4 & 2 YEARS OLD, SENT TO THE LEFT

WEISZ IGNAC-JICCHAK ABOUT 65 YEARS OLD, SENT TO THE LEFT
WEISZ IGNAC'S WIFE ABOUT 60 YEARS OLD, SENT TO THE LEFT
WEISZ KAROLIN ABOUT 35 YRS OLD, NOT SURVIVED
WEISZ EDITH ABOUT 33 YEARS OLD, NOT SURVIVED
WEISZ MANCI ABOUT 30 YEARS OLD, NOT SURVIVED
WEISZ IGNAC'S TWO SONS ABOUT 20 AND 28 YEARS OLD, NOT SURVIVED
WEISZ PESZI ABOUT 24 YEARS OLD, SURVIVED
WEISZ PERKO ABOUT 26 YEARS OLD, SURVIVED
WEISZ'S THREE DAUGHTERS KAROLIN, EDITH AND MANCI WERE MARRIED THEIR SPOUSES AND THEIR CHILDREN, NOT SURVIVED
WEISZ IGNAC'S 28 YEARS OLD, SON AND HIS FAMILY, NOT SURVIVED

WEINBERGER AVROM-LEIB ABOUT 70 YEARS OLD, SENT TO THE LEFT
WEINBERGER'S WIFE ABOUT 65 YEARS OLD, SENT TO THE LEFT

WEISZ MAJSE-BER ABOUT 71 YEARS OLD, SENT TO THE LEFT
WEISZ MAJSE'S WIFE ABOUT 68 YEARS OLD, SENT TO THE LEFT
WEISZ'S MAJSE'S TWO MARRIED DAUGHTERS, THEIR SPOUSES AND THEIR SIX YOUNG CHILDREN, NOT SURVIVED

WEISZ ODON ABOUT 50 YEARS OLD, NOT SURVIVED
WEISZ ODON'S WIFE ABOUT 45 YEARS OLD, NOT SURVIVED
WEISZ ODON'S SON ABOUT 19 YEARS OLD, NOT SURVIVED
WEISZ ODON'S STEPDAUGHTERS 10 AND 12 YEARS OLD, SENT TO THE LEFT
WEISZ ABRAHAM-BUMI ABOUT 38 YEARS OLD, NOT SURVIVED
WEISZ ABRAHAM'S WIFE ABOUT 36 YEARS OLD, NOT SURVIVED
WEISZ'S 3 CHILDREN ABOUT 10, 8, & 6 YEARS OLD, SENT TO THE LEFT

WEISZ ABOUT 70 YEARS OLD, SENT TO THE LEFT
WEISZ'S WIFE ABOUT 68 YEARS OLD, SENT TO THE LEFT
WEISZ'S THREE SONS ABOUT 28, 31 AND 36 YEARS OLD, NOT SURVIVED
WEISZ'S DAUGHTER ABOUT 26 YEARS OLD, NOT SURVIVED
WEISZ'S SONS' & DAUGHTER'S SPOUSES AND FOUR CHILDREN, NOT SURVIVED

ZAUBERER'S WIDOW IREN ABOUT 60 YEARS OLD, NOT SURVIVED
ZAUBERER'S SON ABOUT 31 YEARS OLD, NOT SURVIVED
ZAUBERRE'S SON ABOUT 27 YEARS OLD, SURVIVED
ZAUBERER'S DAUGHTER 24 YEARS OLD, SURVIVED

IN THE 1940'S THERE WERE ABOUT 2000 JEWS IN SIMLEUL-SILVANIEI. THIS LIST DOES NOT CONTAIN ALL OF THEM.

In Memory of My Relatives

In the memory of my grandmother, aunts, uncles, and cousins who were deported from Marghita May/June 1944 to Auschwitz-Birkenau. They were gassed and burned in one of the four crematoriums.

FARKAS-FRIEDMAN LINA 72 YEARS OLD, SENT TO THE LEFT
FRIED-FARKAS GIZELLA 35 YEARS OLD, SENT TO THE LEFT
FRIED ADOLF 37 YEARS OLD, NOT SURVIVE
FRIED SANY 11 YEARS OLD, SENT TO THE LEFT

FARKAS LAJOS 50 YEARS OLD, NOT SURVIVED
FARKAS-HELPERIN ROZSI 48 YEARS OLD, SENT TO THE LEFT
FARKAS BARNABAS 20 YEARS OLD, NOT SURVIVED
FARKAS IBI-VIOLET 18 YEARS OLD, SURVIVED
FARKAS EVA17 YEARS OLD, SURVIVED

ROSENFELD ARMIN 50 YEARS OLD, SENT TO THE LEFT
ROSENFEDL-FARKAS MATILD 48 YEARS OLD, SENT TO THE LEFT
ROSENFELD LALI 24 YEARS OLD, (IN PALESTINE)

MARVANYKOVI MARTON 49 YEARS OLD, SENT TO THE LEFT
MARVANYKOVY-FARKAS ROZSI 46 YEARS OLD, SENT TO THE LEFT
MARVANYKOVI LILI 18 YEARS OLD, SURVIVED
MARVANYKOVI TIBI 29 YEARS OLD, SURVIVED
MARVANYKOVY OCSI 15 YEARS OLD, SENT TO THE LEFT

OTHER DISTANT RELATIVES
DEPORTED FROM UJLACUL DE SIMLEUL (SOMLYOUJLAK)
MAY/JUNE 1944

FRIED JOZSEF 72 YEARS OLD, SENT TO THE LEFT
FRIED-LEOB 70 YEARS OLD SENT TO THE LEFT
FRIED FERENC 43 YEAR OLD, NOT SURVIVED
FRIED JENO 41 YEAR OLD, NOT SURVIVED
FRIED-LEB IREN 30 YEAR OLD, SURVIVED
FRIED IREN HUSBAND BRISTICER LEB 30 YEARS OLD, NOT SURVIVED

DEPORTED FROM NUSFALAU (NAGYFALU) MAY/JUNE 1944
(RELATIVES OF AGNETA'S HUSBAND, T. WEISZ,)

WEISZ ABRAHAM 60 YEAR OLD, SENT TO THE LEFT
WEISZ-IZIK MARGOT 56 YEAR OLD, SENT TO THE LEFT
WEISZ EUGEN 13 YEAR OLD, SENT TO THE LEFT
WEISZ SMILU 19 YEARS OLD, SURVIVED
WEISZ'S THREE DAUGHTERS, IN HIDING SURVIVED

DEPORTED FROM VALEA-LUI-MIHALY (ERMIHALYFALVA)
MAY/JUNE 1944

ROTH ALEX 50 YEARS OLD, SENT TO THE LEFT
ROTH HELEN 46 YEARS OLD, SENT TO THE LEFT
ROTH IRENKE 17 YEARS OLD, NOT SURVIVED
ROTH FERENC 15 YEARS OLD, SENT TO THE LEFT
ROTH IDA 13 YEARS OLD, SENT TO THE LEFT
ROTH'S OTHER SON 11 YEARS OLD, SENT TO THE LEFT

KIBOVICS LENKE 36 YEARS OLD, NOT SURVIVED
KIBOVICS EDITH 17 YEARS OLD, NOT SURVIVED

In Memory of My Husband's Relatives

My husband's mother, Hermina Gross, passed away in 1937. His other close family relatives were deported in the spring of 1944. Due to his stroke, Ernest is unable to remember their exact ages and the names of other relatives.

MARTIN GROSS 74 YEARS OLD (FATHER)
GEZA, KAPI (BROTHERS) ROZSI, ILONA (SISTERS)
THEIR SPOUSES AND CHILDREN ALL PERISHED
ALADAR, ERNEST, BELLA, AND JOLAN SURVIVED.

Acknowledgements

My appreciation to my friend Mrs. Rose Boord. She tirelessly corrected my vocabulary in order for my readers to have a better understanding of my English. Without her this and the previous book never would have been published. Unfortunately I was not lucky enough to be born in the United States of America. I learned English late in my life.

Gratefully my deepest thanks to Ms. Marsha Hoffer, Production Manager at Columbia House Company and Andrew Gerber, Esq. of Columbia House Company who assisted in the "pro-bono" printing of my first book, "Poems of Elly Gross, Memories of A Holocaust Survivor" (ISBN 0-9713639-0-0).

Forever my gratitude for their kindness. A simple word "Thanks" is not enough to express my feelings.

Storm Against the Innocents, Holocaust Memories and Other Stories (ISBN 0-9713639-1-9).

For this book, Marsha Hoffer is manager, organizer and editor. Without her continuous devotion and assistance my second book would not have been printed.

Art Directed by Katerina Caterisano and Jill Davis of Network Design Studio in NYC.

Jacket Design by Katerina Caterisano.
Layout by Eddie Largo.

Photos burned to CD by Moon Lee Photography in NYC.

Permission to quote June Jordan on Back Cover granted by the Literary Estate of June M. Jordan.

Photo Credits

Except where noted, photos are selected from the Author's collection of over 800 pictures she took during visits to the killing fields and other sites. Additional photos are from pictures from the family album and also from visits to the World Trade Center site. Collages and paintings by Author.

Use of photos taken of displays at the camps Auschwitz-I and Auschwitz-II/Birkenau and map authorized by Archives Director of the Panstwowe Muzeum Oswiecimiu, (Auschwitz-Birkenau). Permission to use photos, L.dz.I.Arch-61/1076/2003 Panstwowe Muzeum Oswiecimiu L.dz.I-Arch-68/1131/03 4-5, 7-18 neg. no. 20992/145, 817, 522, 20995/412, 485, 18938, 12709, 32, 41, 90, 141, 295, 296, 280, 540, L.dz. I-Arch-580/03.®

Page viii: Remembrance Page: Original photo of attack on the World Trade Center by Mr. Neil Robert Berzak. © Berzak (photo #1990)

Pages ix and 86: photos of Pope John II. gpophoto@netvision.net.il, D608-038 and D612-065 (authorization #605)

Page 141: Use of "Maurers Schwedenbitter" label authorized by the Maurers Krautergarten GMBH, Klagenfurt, Austria

Page 167: "Liberation 1945" (Ebensee Concentration Camp). Photo in the public domain #66297 or the property of the USHNN. See page 167 for add'l details.

Pages 168-169: Auschwitz map.

Pages 170-171: Reproduction of web page authorized by Yad Vashem, The Holocaust Martyrs' and Heroes' Remembrance Authority. www.yadvashem.org.